the *little book* of
BABY NAMES

the little book of BABY NAMES

Marissa Charles

ARCTURUS

ARCTURUS

This edition published in 2012 by Arcturus Publishing Limited
26/27 Bickels Yard, 151–153 Bermondsey Street,
London SE1 3HA

ISBN: 978-1-84858-397-9
AD002100EN

Printed in China

Introduction

Choosing a name, or names, for your baby is one of the hardest decisions you'll make in your life. For a name is so much more than just a label, a means of identifying your child from everybody else's. The name you bestow on your child reflects your personality and beliefs and, as time goes by, you hope it will reflect theirs.

But you are spoilt for choice. There are so many names in use – and, of course, you can always make up a brand new one. So where do you start? It always helps to learn a bit about the names you like, as their origin can be a further source of inspiration. Including variants, this book contains well over 3,000 names for boys and girls, each with its origin explained.

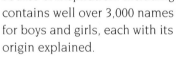

Included are many names that have become popular in recent years, along with some all-time favourites that have been used in some form or other for thousands of years! There are names from the Bible, from Sanskrit, names used by the Native American Indians and the tribes of Africa – and, of course, the traditional names of the English-speaking peoples, derived from Greek, Latin, Germanic, Gaelic and Old English.

The aim of this book is to help you enjoy choosing your baby's name – and ensure that you make a choice that everyone is happy with!

Girls'
Names

Aaliyah
Arabic and Hebrew in origin, this name means 'to ascend', 'highly exalted' and 'tall or towering'. Also possibly derived from the biblical Aliya, which means 'defender'.

Abigail
Derived from the Hebrew name Avigayil, which means 'father rejoiced', 'source of joy'.
VARIANTS: Abagael, Abbie, Abby, Abagael, Abigael, Abigayle

Abira
A Hebrew name meaning 'strong' and 'heroic'.
VARIANTS: Adira, Amiza

Ada
The Latin version of the biblical Adah, which means 'lovely ornament', or from the Old English for 'happy' and the Old German for 'noble and kind'.
VARIANTS: Adah, Adda, Addie, Addy, Adele, Aeda, Aida, Eada, Eda, Etta

Adelaide
The French form of the Old German for 'noble' and 'sort', and a city in Australia.
VARIANTS: Ada, Adalhaide, Adalia, Adda, Addi, Addison, Adélaïde, Adelina, Heidi

Adelpha
From the Greek meaning 'sisterly' or 'sister to mankind'.

Adesina
Families from the Yoruba tribe in West Africa give this name to their first baby. It means 'my arrival opens the way for more'.

Adiel
In Hebrew this name means 'ornament of the Lord'.
VARIANTS: Adie, Adiell, Adiella

Aditi
A Hindi name meaning 'free abundance' or 'unbounded creativity'.

Adrienne
From the Latin meaning 'dark one' or 'black, mysterious one'. In Greek, Adrienne means 'rich'.
VARIANTS: Adrea, Adria, Adriana, Adriane, Adrianna, Adrien, Adrienne, Hadria, Riana

Aida
In Latin and Old French Aida comes from words meaning 'to help, assist'. In Greek it means 'modesty', in Arabic it means 'reward' and the Old English interpretation is 'happy'.
VARIANTS: Aidan, Iraida, Zaida, Zenaida, Zoraida

Aine
The queen of the fairies in Irish mythology, Aine means 'little fire'.

Aisha
A biblical name from the Arabic 'woman', 'prospering' or 'alive and well'.
VARIANTS: Aesha, Aishali, Asha, Asia, Ayasha, Ayesha, Aysha

Alexandra

A name from Greek mythology meaning 'defender'.
VARIANTS: Alessandra, Alex, Alexandria, Alexandrina, Alexandrine, Alexia, Lexie, Xandra

Alice

Originally a pet form of the German name Adelaide, which means 'noble'.
VARIANTS: Alicia, Allie, Alli, Allis, Alissa, Alix, Alys, Alyssa

Alison

Like Alice and Adelaide, Alison means 'noble'.
VARIANTS: Allie, Allison, Ally

Alma

From the Latin word 'almus', which means 'nourishing, kind', Alma also has meanings in Hebrew ('maiden'), Italian ('soul'), Spanish ('warm-hearted'), Turkish ('apple') and Celtic ('all good').
VARIANTS: Aluma, Alumit, Elma

Almita

Of Latin origin, meaning 'benign' or 'kindly behaviour'.

Amalia

A variant of Amelia, from the Latin for 'toil'.
VARIANTS: Amaliah, Amalie, Amalthea, Amelia

Amanda

Derived from the Latin for 'worthy of love' or 'loveable'.
VARIANTS: Amandine, Amata, Manda, Mandi, Mandie, Mandy

Amarinda

Of Greek origin, meaning 'long-lived'.
VARIANTS: Amara, Amargo, Mara

Amber

Both a colour and a gemstone, Amber comes from the Arabic word for 'jewel'.
VARIANTS: Amberlea, Amberlee, Amberline, Amberly, Ambur, Amby

Ambrosia

The Greek word 'ambrosios' means 'immortality' and 'elixir of life'.
VARIANTS: Ambrosina, Ambrosine

Amelia

The Latin meaning of Amelia is 'industrious'. The name may also come from the Latin 'aemilia', which means 'persuasive and flattering'.
VARIANTS: Amalea, Amalia, Amalie, Ameline, Emelita, Emil, Emilia, Emily

Amethyst

A violet gemstone, from the Greek word for 'intoxicated'.

Amina

Rooted in both Arabic and Hebrew, meaning 'truth, certainty' and 'affirmation'.

Amorette

From the Latin for 'beloved' meaning 'little dear'.
VARIANT: Amorita

Amy

A variant of the French Aimée, from the Latin for 'love'.
VARIANTS: Aimee, Aimée, Amata, Ame, Ami, Esme, Esmee, Ismay

Anais

A French name from the Greek for 'fruitful'.

Anastasia

A Russian name from the Greek for 'resurrection' or 'one who will rise again'.
VARIANTS: Ana, Anastas, Annestas, Anstes, Anstis, Nastia, Stasa, Tansy, Tasya

Andrea

The feminine form of Andrew, from the Greek meaning 'manly'.
VARIANTS: Andreana, Andrée, Andreena, Andrene, Andrina, Dreena, Rena

Anemone

From the Greek for 'wind flower'.

Angel

From the Greek for 'a messenger from God'.
VARIANTS: Angela, Angeles, Angelica, Angelina, Angelique, Angie

Angela

A variant of Angel.

Annabel

A compound of Anna (Hebrew for 'God has favoured me') and 'belle' (French for 'beautiful').
VARIANTS: Annabella, Annabelle

Anne

A variant of the biblical name Hannah, which means 'God has favoured me'.
VARIANTS: Anika, Anita, Ann, Anna, Annalise, Anneka, Annette, Annias, Anoushka, Nanette, Nansi, Nina, Ninette

Anthea

From the Greek word for 'flowery'.
VARIANT: Anthia

Antoinette
From the Roman family name Antonius, meaning 'without price'.
VARIANTS: Antonetta, Antonette, Antonia, Toinette, Toni, Tonneli

Aphrodite
The Greek goddess of love, fertility and beauty, the name is said to mean 'foam born' because she came to life by rising from the sea.

April
The month of April gets its name from the Latin 'to open' or 'to open to the sun'.
VARIANTS: Aprilette, Averyl, Avril

Arabella
A Scottish name of Latin origin, which means 'moved by prayer'.
VARIANTS: Ara, Arabel, Arabela, Arabelle, Arable, Arbel, Orabell, Orable

Aria
From the Latin for 'melody', 'air' and 'tune'.

Ariana
Rooted in both Greek and Welsh, meaning 'holy', 'holy one' and 'silver'.

Ashanti
The name of a West African tribe that once ruled a great empire.
VARIANTS: Asante, Shante

Ashley
Originally a surname, derived from the Old English for 'ash' and 'wood'.
VARIANTS: Ashlea, Ashlee, Ashleigh, Ashlie, Ashly, Ashlynn, Ashton

Atlanta
A city in the USA, the name comes from Atalanta, the feminine form of Atlas, from Greek mythology.
VARIANT: Atalanta

Audrey
A variant of the Old English Etheldreda, meaning 'noble strength'.
VARIANTS: Addie, Addy, Atheldreda, Aude, Audey, Audra, Audrie, Awdrie, Ethel, Etheldreda

Aura
Of Greek origin, meaning 'gentle breeze'.
VARIANT: Awal

Aurora
From the Latin for 'dawn'.
VARIANTS: Alola, Aurore, Ora, Rora, Rori, Rorie, Rory

Ava
A variant of Eve, which means 'living', or from the Latin 'avis', meaning 'bird'.
VARIANTS: Eva, Eve

Avalon
According to Arthurian legend, Avalon was the island to which King Arthur was taken after his death. The name comes from the Latin for 'island', but also from the Old Welsh for 'apple'.
VARIANT: Avallon

Bailey
Originally a surname, either for a bailiff or someone who lived near a city fortification.
VARIANTS: Bailee, Baileigh, Bailie, Baily, Baylee, Bayleigh, Baylie

Barbara
Of Greek origin, meaning 'foreign' or 'strange'.
VARIANTS: Bab, Babette, Babs, Barbra, Baubie, Bobbi, Bobbie

Beatrice
From the Latin for 'blessed' or 'blessings', but also derived from the Latin name Viatrix, which means 'voyager'.
VARIANTS: Bea, Beah, Beate, Beatrise, Beatrix, Bebe, Bee, Trixie, Trixy

Belinda
A combination of the Latin 'bel', for 'beautiful', and the Old German 'linda', for 'a snake or serpent', a symbol of wisdom.
VARIANTS: Bel, Bell, Bellalinda, Bindy, Blenda, Linda, Lindi, Line, Lynda, Lynde

Belle
The French word for 'beautiful'.
VARIANTS: Bel, Bela, Bell, Bill, Billi, Billie

Bena
From the Hebrew for 'wise'.
VARIANTS: Bina, Buna, Bunie

Bernadette
The French feminine form of Bernard, a German name that means 'strong, brave as a bear'.
VARIANTS: Berna, Bernarda, Bernadina, Bernette, Bernita

Bernice
A variant of the biblical Berenice, from the Greek for 'bringer of victory'.
VARIANTS: Berenice, Bernelle, Bernine, Bernita, Bunni, Bunnie, Pherenice, Vernice

Bess
A pet form of Elizabeth, meaning 'God is perfection'.
VARIANTS: Bessie, Bessy

Bethany
A Hebrew name, which means 'house of figs'.

Betsy
Another pet form of Elizabeth.
VARIANT: Betsie

Bette

Pronounced either 'Bet' or 'Betty', Bette is another short form of Elizabeth.
VARIANTS: Betsie, Betsy, Bettie, Bettina, Betty

Beverley

From the Old English for 'beaver's meadow' or 'beaver's stream'.
VARIANTS: Beverlee, Beverly, Buffy

Bianca

From the Italian for 'white' or 'pure'.
VARIANTS: Biancha, Bibi, Blanche

Bibi

From the French 'beubelot', which means 'toy' or 'bauble'. Also a short form of Bianca.

Bijou

From the French for 'jewel'.

Billie

A feminine version of William, from the Germanic Wilhelm.
VARIANTS: Bill, Billy

Blair

A Scottish name from the Celtic for 'place', 'field' or 'battle'.
VARIANTS: Blaire, Blayre

Blaise

From the Old English for 'torch' or 'shining' and the Middle English for 'proclaim' and 'to blow'.
VARIANT: Blaze

Blanche

A variant of Bianca, meaning 'white'.
VARIANTS: Balaniki, Bellanca, Bianca, Blanca, Blanch

Bliss

From Old English meaning 'happiness' and 'joy'.

Blossom

From the Old English for 'flower'.
VARIANTS: Blom, Bloom, Blum, Bluma

Blythe

In Old English 'blithe' means 'mild', 'gentle' and 'kind'.
VARIANTS: Bliss, Blisse

Bo

From the Chinese for 'precious' and also the Old Norse meaning 'house-owner'.
VARIANT: Bonita

Bobbie

A pet form of Barbara and Roberta.
VARIANTS: Bobbi, Bobby

Bonita

A Spanish name meaning 'pretty little one'.
VARIANTS: Boni, Bonie, Bonnie, Bonny, Nita

Bonnie

An old Scottish name meaning 'pretty'.
VARIANTS: Bonita, Bonnee, Bonni, Bonny

Brandy

A feminine form of Brandon, from the Old English for 'broom' and 'hill', or from the Middle English for 'torch', 'fire' or 'sword'.
VARIANTS: Brandee, Brandi, Brandie

Breanna

The feminine equivalent of the Celtic boys' name Brian.
VARIANTS: Breanne, Breeanna, Brenna, Bria, Brianna

Brenda

A short form of the Old Norse word 'brand', meaning 'sword'.
VARIANTS: Bren, Brenna

Bridget

The ancient Celtic goddess of fire, light and poetry, Bridget means 'strength' and 'high one', while the Scandinavian interpretation is 'protection'.
VARIANTS: Biddie, Biddy, Birgit, Bridie, Brigette, Brigid, Brigitte, Britt

Britney

A variant of Brittany, meaning 'from Britain'.
VARIANTS: Britany, Brittanie, Brittany, Brittnee, Brittney, Brittni

Bronwyn

Of Welsh origin, Bronwyn means 'fair bosomed'.
VARIANTS: Bron, Bronnie, Bronny, Bronwen

Brook

From the Old English for a 'stream' or 'to enjoy, be rewarded by'.
VARIANTS: Brooke, Brooklynn, Brooklynne

Bryony

A variant of the Greek name for a wild climbing plant, which means 'to grow luxuriantly'.
VARIANT: Briony

Caitlín
Pronounced 'kat-leen',
Caitlín is the Irish Gaelic
version of Catherine,
which comes from the
Greek for 'pure'.
VARIANTS: Caitlin, Kaitlyn,
Kaitlynn, Katelyn, Katelynn

Calista
From the Greek meaning
'most beautiful'.
VARIANTS: Calesta, Calisto,
Calla, Calli, Callie

Camilla
Derived from the Roman
family name Camillus,
which means 'messenger'.
VARIANTS: Cam, Camala,
Camel, Camila, Camille,
Cammie, Milli, Millie, Milly

Caprice
Originally from an Italian
word meaning 'with hair
standing on end', this
has come to mean
'fanciful, whimsical'.
Associated with the star
sign Capricorn.

Carlene
A variant of Carla and
Karla, which are feminine
forms of Charles.
VARIANTS: Carla, Carleen,
Carly, Carlyn, Carol, Karla

Carmel
A mountain in Israel
that is mentioned in the
Bible, from the Hebrew for
'garden' or 'orchard'.
VARIANTS: Carmela,
Carmelina

Carmen
The Spanish form of
Carmel, its Latin meaning
is 'to sing, praise' and
'be lyrical'.
VARIANTS: Carmia,
Carmine, Charmaine,
Charmione

Carol
From the Old German for
'free man' or 'man', as the
feminine form of Charles.
Also linked to the Welsh
for 'brave in battle' and
the Old French for
'round dance'.
VARIANTS: Carey, Carrie,
Carola, Carolee, Carole,
Carroll, Caroline, Carolyn,
Cary, Caryl

Carrie
A short form of Carol and
Caroline, but also from
the Welsh word for 'love'.
VARIANTS: Cari, Carin,
Carine, Carol, Carole,
Caryn, Carys, Ceri, Cerys

Catherine
From the Greek word
for 'pure'.
VARIANTS: Caitlín, Carina,
Cathleen, Cathy, Kate,
Katerina, Katharine,
Katherine, Kathryn, Katie

Cecilia
A saint's name from the
Welsh for 'sixth' and
the Latin for 'blind'.
VARIANTS: Cacile, Cacilia,
Celia, Cecile, Cecily, Cicely,
Cissie, Cissy, Sissy

Cerys
From the Welsh word
for 'love'.
VARIANTS: Cari, Caryl,
Carys

Chandra
From the Sanskrit for
'illustrious' or 'like
the moon'.
VARIANTS: Chan, Chandah,
Shan, Shandra

Chanel
French for 'channel' or
'canal', this has been made
popular by the fashion
designer Coco Chanel.
VARIANTS: Chanelle,
Shanell, Shannel

Chantelle

From the French for 'to sing' or 'candle'.
VARIANTS: Chantal, Chantel, Shantal, Shantel, Shantell, Shantelle

Chardonnay

The name of a white wine grape (or a character in UK TV series 'Footballers' Wives'), this was first used to call girls by in the USA in the 1980s.

Charity

From Charis, the Greek goddess of beauty and grace.
VARIANTS: Charito, Karis

Charlotte

The French feminine form of Charles.
VARIANTS: Cara, Charlayne, Charleen, Charlie, Lottie

Charmaine

Derived from the older name Charmian, from the Greek for 'joy' or the Latin for 'song'.
VARIANTS: Carman, Charmain, Charmayne, Charmian, Sharmaine, Sharmayne

Chelsea

An English place name, from the Old English meaning 'chalk landing place'.
VARIANTS: Chelsi, Chelsie

Chenoa

A Native American name meaning 'white dove'.

Chere

A French word meaning 'dear' or 'beloved'
VARIANTS: Cher, Cherami, Cherie, Cherri, Cherrie, Cherry, Cheryl, Cherylie

Cherry

A pet form of Charity, but also a fruit, possibly from the French for 'beloved'.

Cheryl

A variant of Cherry, meaning 'dear, beloved'.
VARIANTS: Chère, Sheralyn, Sherrell, Sheryl

China

Like India and Kenya, this country's name is gaining popularity as a girl's name.
VARIANTS: Chynna

Chloë

From the Greek word for 'green' or a 'young green shoot'.
VARIANT: Chloe

Christabel

A combination of Christine with the suffix 'bel', meaning 'beautiful Christian'.
VARIANTS: Bell, Bel, Christa, Christabell, Christabella, Christabelle, Christable, Christie, Christobella

Christina

A female version of Christian, meaning 'follower of Christ'.
VARIANTS: Chris, Chrissie, Christiana, Christine, Kirstie, Kirsty, Krista, Kristen, Kristine, Krystyna, Tina, Xena

Christine

Another female form of Christian.
VARIANTS: Chris, Chrissie, Kersten, Kirsten, Kirstie, Kirsty, Krista, Kristen, Kristine

Cindy

A short form of Cynthia (the Greek moon goddess), Lucinda (Latin for 'light') and Cinderella (from the French for 'ashes').
VARIANTS: Cindi, Cyndi, Sindy, Syndi

Claire

Derived from the Latin for 'bright, clear' and 'famous'.
VARIANTS: Clair, Clare, Claribel, Clarrie

Clara

Like Claire, from the Latin word for 'bright, clear' and 'famous'.
VARIANTS: Clara-Mae, Claribelle, Clarinda

Claudette

The French feminine form of Claude, from the Latin word 'claudus', which means 'lame'.
VARIANT: Claudia

Cleo

The pet form of Cleopatra, meaning 'glory of her father'.
VARIANTS: Cleopatra, Clio

Clove
A spice, which takes its name from the Latin for 'nail'.

Clover
An Old English word for a plant associated with good luck.

Coco
A nickname, made popular by fashion designer Coco Chanel.
VARIANT: Koko

Colleen
From the Irish Gaelic word for 'girl'.
VARIANTS: Coleen, Colena, Colene, Coline, Collene, Collice

Colette
A French feminine variant of Nicholas, from the Greek for 'victory of the people'.
VARIANTS: Colet, Collette, Cosetta, Cosette, Kalotte

Connie
Short for Constance, a virtue derived from the Roman emperor Constantine.
VARIANTS: Conetta, Constance, Constanza

Consuela
From the Latin meaning 'to free from sadness'.
VARIANTS: Consolata, Consuelo

Cora
Possibly a derivative of the Greek word 'kore', which means 'maiden'.
VARIANTS: Corabelle, Coretta, Corette, Corinna, Corinne, Kora

Coral
An ornament, derived from the Greek word for 'pebble', or a short form of the French name Coralie.
VARIANTS: Coralie, Coraline

Cori
Originally a surname, derived from an Old English word for 'helmet'.
VARIANTS: Corey, Corie, Cory, Korey, Kori, Korie, Kory

Corina
From the Greek word 'kore', which means 'maiden'.
VARIANTS: Cora, Corene, Cori, Corinna

Courtney
A French place name meaning 'short nose', and also an English name that means 'from the court' or 'member of the court'.
VARIANTS: Cortney, Courteney, Kortney, Korteney

Crystal
From the Greek word 'krystallos', which means 'ice'.
VARIANTS: Christel, Chrystal, Krystal, Krystle

Cynthia
Derived from 'Mount Cynthus', the birthplace of Greek goddesses.
VARIANTS: Cindi, Cindy, Cynth, Sindi, Sindy

Cyr
A feminine form of Cyril, from the Greek word for 'lord'.
VARIANTS: Ciri, Cirilla, Cyra, Cyrilla

Daffodil

A bright yellow flower, the name is Dutch, from the Greek 'asphodel'.
VARIANTS: Daff, Daffie, Daffy, Dilly

Dahlia

Another colourful flower, named after the Swedish botanist Anders Dahl.
VARIANTS: Dahla, Dalia, Daliah

Daisy

From the Old English for 'day's eye', a reference to the way the petals open in the morning and close at night. Daisy is also a pet form of Margaret because of its association with a saint.

Dakota

North and South Dakota are two states in the USA, which took their name from the Dakota division of the Sioux tribe. It means 'friend'.

Dallas

Also a surname as well as a city in Texas, Dallas was originally a place name in England and Scotland meaning 'house or dwelling in the valley'.

Damaris

A Biblical name from the Greek for either 'calf' or 'gentle'.
VARIANTS: Damara, Damaras, Damaress, Damiris, Mara, Mari, Maris

Dana

As a female form of Daniel, Dana means 'God has judged' or 'God is my judge'. But it can also come from the Old English for 'a Dane', or from the Irish Gaelic for 'bold' or 'courageous'. Dana was the Celtic goddess of fertility.
VARIANTS: Daina, Danae, Dane, Dania, Danice, Danita, Danna, Danni

Danielle

The French, feminine form of Daniel, meaning 'God is my judge'.
VARIANTS: Dani, Daniella, Danii

Daphne

A character from Greek mythology, whose name means 'laurel or bay tree'.
VARIANTS: Daff, Daffie, Daffy, Dafna, Dafnee, Daphna, Daphnee

Darcie

A contraction of the Norman d'Arcy ('from Arcy'). Also an Anglicised form of an Irish name that means 'descendant of the dark one'.
VARIANTS: Dar, Darce, Darci, Darcy, D'Arcy, Darsey

Daria

As the feminine form of the Persian name Darius, it means 'protector' or 'royalty'. Its Greek meaning is 'wealthy, rich'. As a variant of Dara, it comes from the Middle English for 'compassion' and 'to have courage, daring'.
VARIANTS: Dara, Darice, Darya

Darleen

From the Old English for 'darling', 'beloved', 'highly valued, worthy, favourite'.
VARIANTS: Darilyn, Darilynn, Darlene, Darlin, Darline

Daryl

A contraction of the Norman 'd'Airel' ('from Airel').
VARIANTS: Darrel, Darrell, Darryl

Davina

Feminine form of David ('beloved, friend'), Davina originated in Scotland.
VARIANTS: Davene, Davi, Davida, Davinia, Davita, Devina

Dawn

From the Old English word for 'daybreak'.
VARIANTS: Aurora, Dawne, Dawnelle, Orrie, Rora

Dayanara

From Deianeira, wife of Hercules.
VARIANTS: Deja, Delaneiria, Diya

Deborah

A biblical name from the Hebrew for 'bee'.
VARIANTS: Deb, Debbi, Debbie, Debby, Debora, Debra, Debs

Dee

Short for any name that begins with the letter 'D'. Also a Welsh name from the word for 'dark' or 'black'.
VARIANTS: DD, Dede, DeeDee, Didi

Delia

A Greek name that originally meant 'girl from Delos'.
VARIANTS: Dede, Dee, Dehlia, Delinda, Della, Didi

Delilah

This famous biblical name means 'full of desire' and also comes from the Arabic for 'guide, leader'.

Delwyn

A compound of the Welsh words 'del' ('pretty, neat') and '(g)wyn' ('white, fair' or 'blessed and holy').
VARIANT: Del

Delwyth

From the Welsh for 'pretty' and 'neat', with the suffix 'yth' meaning 'lovely'.
VARIANT: Del

Denna

As a feminine form of the name Dean, Denna means 'valley'. Also a variant of Diana, the Roman goddess of the moon.
VARIANTS: Dea, Deana, Deanna, Deanne, Diana

Dervla

Anglicised version of the Gaelic name Deirbhile, meaning 'daughter of the poet'.
VARIANTS: Dearbhla, Derval, Dervilia

Desiree

A French name meaning 'desired' or 'longed for'.
VARIANTS: Desarae, Desaree, Desi, Desideria, Desire, Désirée, Deziree

Destiny

This alternative word for 'fate' has found popularity as a given name in North America.
VARIANTS: Destinee, Destiney, Destinie

Deva

The name of a goddess in both Hindu and Celtic religions.
VARIANTS: Devaki, Devanee, Devi, Devika, Dewi

Devon

The name of an English county, from the Celtic Dumnoni tribe that settled there.
VARIANTS: Davon, Devan, Deven, Devonne

Dextra

From the Latin for 'right-hand side', from which we get 'dextrous', meaning skilful.

Diamond

The clear, precious stone takes its name from the Greek for 'hardest' or 'unconquerable'.
VARIANT: Diamanta

Diana

The name of a Roman goddess, protector of wild animals and goddess of the moon.
VARIANTS: Deanna, Deeanna, Dian, Diandra, Diane, Dianne, Dinah, Dyanna

Diandra

A variant of Diana, possibly blended with Andrea.
VARIANT: Diandrea

Diantha

Of Greek origin, this name means 'heavenly flower'.
VARIANT: Dianthe

Dinah

A Biblical name that means 'vindication', 'judgement' or 'revenged'.
VARIANTS: Deanna, Deanne, Deena, Dena, Diana, Dina

Dixie

A reference to Dixieland, the nickname for the southern states of the USA. Dixie may also come from the Old Norse word 'diss', which means 'active sprite'.
VARIANTS: Dis, Disa, Dix

Dolcila

From the Latin word 'dolcilis', which means 'gentle' and 'amenable'.
VARIANTS: Docila, Docilla

Dolly

A pet form of Dorothy, which means 'God's gift'.
VARIANT: Doll

Dolores

From the Spanish word for 'sorrows', historically used as an alternative to Mary.
VARIANTS: Dalores, Dela, Delora, Delores, Deloris, Delorita, Dola, Dolore, Lola, Lolita

Dominique

The feminine form of Dominic, from the Latin for 'of the Lord', traditionally given to babies born on a Sunday. The name is also thought to mean 'servant of God'.

Donna

The Italian word for 'lady', and a short form of Madonna.
VARIANTS: Dona, Donalie, Donella, Donelle, Donica, Donnis, Donny, Ladonna

Dorothy

From the Greek Dorothea, which means 'gift of God'.
VARIANTS: Dolly, Dora, Dorrit, Dot, Dotty.

Dove

This white bird is a symbol of peace and gentleness.
VARIANT: Dova

Drew

This short form of the name Andrew ('manly') is also a girl's name.

Dulcie

Derived from the Latin 'dulcis', which means 'sweet'.
VARIANTS: Dowsabel, Dulce, Dulcee, Dulcia, Dulcy

Dymphna

An Irish Gaelic name meaning 'eligible one' or 'little fawn'.
VARIANTS: Damhnait, Dympna

Easter
From the Middle English for 'ester', which means 'where the sun rises'.
VARIANT: Esther

Ebony
From the word for the black, hard wood of a tropical tree.
VARIANTS: Ebbony, Eboney, Eboni, Ebonie

Echo
The name of a nymph from Greek mythology who could only repeat what others had said.

Eileen
The Anglicised form of the Irish Gaelic Aibhilin, which in turn was derived from the Norman French name Aveline, meaning 'hazelnut'. Eileen is also thought to be an Irish variant of Helen, from the Greek for 'bright'.
VARIANTS: Aibhilin, Aileen, Eilleen, Elly, Evelyn, Helen, Ileen, Ileene

Elaine
From the Old French form of Helen ('bright'), or from the Welsh for 'fawn'.
VARIANTS: Elain, Elaina, Elane, Elayne, Eleanor, Ellaine, Helen

Eleanor
An Old French variant of Helen ('bright'), and also a derivative of the Old Provençal name Alienor, from the German for 'foreign'.
VARIANTS: Elenor, Elenora, Ella, Elle, Ellie, Elyn, Helen, Nell, Nora, Norah

Electra
From the Greek 'elektron', which means 'amber one that shines brightly'.
VARIANTS: Electre, Elektra

Elisha
A feminine derivative of the biblical name Eli, meaning 'God saves', as well as a combination of Elise and Alicia, to mean 'God's oath' and 'noble'.
VARIANTS: Alicia, Elisa, Elise

Elizabeth
From the Hebrew Elisheva, which means 'God's oath' or the 'fullness of God'.
VARIANTS: Bess, Bessie, Bet, Beth, Betsy, Betty, Elisa, Elise, Eliza, Elsa, Libby, Liesel, Lilibet, Lisa, Lisbeth, Liza

Ella
Of both Old English and Old German origin, Ella means either 'fairy maiden' or 'all'. Also a pet form of Eleanor and Isabella.
VARIANTS: Ala, Eleanor, Ellen, Isabella

Ellie
A short form of any name beginnng 'El', as well as Alice, Adelaide and Alicia.
VARIANTS: Adelaide, Alice, Alicia, Ella, Elle, Eleanor, Elizabeth

Elma
This means 'apple' in Turkish and 'amiable' in Greek.

Elsa

As the Scottish short form of the biblical name Elizabeth, Elsa means 'God's oath'.
VARIANTS: Aliza, Elizabeth, Else, Elsie, Elza

Emerald

From the Latin word for the green gem stone.
VARIANTS: Emeralda, Emeraldine, Esmeralda

Emily

Derived from the medieval form of the Latin name Aemilia. Also related to the Germanic name Amelia, which means 'industrious'.
VARIANTS: Amelia, Amelie, Em, Emma, Emmie, Emilie

Emma

Originally the short form of names containing the German element 'ermin', e.g. Ermintrude ('universal strength').
VARIANTS: Em, Ema, Emily, Emm, Emmie, Emmy, Irma

Enya

An Irish name meaning 'small fire'. Also a variant of Eithne, which means 'kernel'.
VARIANT: Ena, Eithne

Erica

The feminine form of the Viking name Eric, which means 'eternal', 'honourable', 'alone' and 'ruler'. In Latin Erica means 'heather'.
VARIANTS: Ericka, Erika, Rica, Ricki

Erin

A poetic name for Ireland, which also means 'peace'.
VARIANT: Errin

Esmé

From the French for 'esteemed'.
VARIANTS: Aimee, Aimée, Esma, Esme, Esmee

Estelle

Derived from the Old French for 'star'.
VARIANTS: Essie, Estella, Esther, Stella

Eternity

A word of Old French origin, meaning 'everlasting'.

Etta

Short for both Henrietta ('home rule') and Rosetta ('rose').

Eugenie

The French feminine form of Eugene, from the Greek for 'excellent', 'well-born' and 'fortunate'.
VARIANTS: Eugenia, Gene, Genie, Ina

Eve

The name of the first woman in the Bible comes from the Hebrew for 'breath of life'.
VARIANTS: Eva, Evadne, Eveleen, Evie, Evita, Zoe

Evelyn

From the Germanic and Old French name Aveline, which means 'hazelnut'.
VARIANTS: Aibhilin, Aileen, Eileen, Eveline, Evelyne

Fabia
The feminine form of the old Roman family name Fabianus, which was derived from the word for 'bean'.

Faith
One of the three major Christian virtues.
VARIANTS: Fay, Faye, Fayth, Faythe, Fidelity

Fallon
Anglicised form of an Irish surname that means 'leader' or 'descendant of the leader'.

Fancy
From the Greek for 'to make visible'.
VARIANT: Fancie

Fanny
A short form of Frances ('Frenchman') and the Welsh name Myfanwy ('my treasure').

Farrah
From the Arabic for 'happiness', 'joy' and 'cheerfulness', as well as from the Middle English for 'lovely', 'beautiful' and 'pleasant'.
VARIANTS: Fara, Farah, Farra

Fatima
An Arabic name meaning 'chaste', 'motherly' and 'abstainer'.
VARIANTS: Fatimah, Fatma

Faustine
Of Italian and Spanish origin, this name means 'fortunate'.

Fawn
Another word for a 'young deer'.
VARIANTS: Fauna, Fawna, Fawnah, Fawniah

Faye

A pet form of Faith, which means 'trust' and 'devotion', and also derived from the Old French word for 'fairy'.
VARIANTS: Fae, Faith, Fay, Fayette

Felicia

From the Roman Felicitas, who was the Roman goddess of happiness and good fortune.
VARIANTS: Falice, Falicia, Felice, Felicity

Felicity

Like Felicia, from the Latin word for 'happiness'.
VARIANTS: Falice, Falicia, Felicie, Felicite

Fenella

Anglicised version of the Gaelic name Fionnghuala, which is made up of the words for 'white, fair' and 'shouldered'.
VARIANTS: Finella, Fionola, Fionnuala, Nuala

Ferelith

A Scottish name from the Old Irish words for 'true, very' and 'lady or princess'.

Fern

Taken from the Old English for 'leaf'.
VARIANT: Fearne, Ferne

Ffion

In medieval love poetry this Welsh name was used to describe the colour and/or softness of a girl's cheek. It also comes from the old Welsh word for foxglove.
VARIANTS: Ffiona, Fionn,

Fifi

A pet form of Josephine, the feminine version of Joseph, which means 'God shall add another'.
VARIANT: Josephine

Filma

From the Old English for 'misty veil'.

Fiona

From the Celtic word for 'white, fair', this is also believed to be a creation of the writer William Sharp, who penned his romantic works under the pseudonym Fiona Macleod.
VARIANTS: Fenella, Finella, Fionola, Fionnuala

Flavia

A Roman dynastic name, from the Latin for 'golden' or 'yellow', pertaining to hair colour.

Fleur

The French word for 'flower'.
VARIANTS: Ffleur, Fflur, Fleurette, Flora, Flower

Floella

A compound of Flo (a diminutive of Florence) and Ella.

Flora

From the Latin for 'flower' or 'blossom'.
VARIANTS: Fflur, Fleur, Fleurette, Flo, Flor, Flores, Florrie, Flossie

Florence

A famous Italian city, named from the Latin for 'blossoming' or 'flourishing'.
VARIANTS: Flo, Flora, Florance, Floreen, Florrie, Flossie, Flossy

Flower

This is the English version of the French name Fleur.
VARIANTS: Fleur, Flora

Frances

Derived from the Old Middle Latin word 'franciscus', which means 'a free man'.
VARIANTS: Fran, France, Francesca, Frankie

Francesca

The Italian version of Frances.
VARIANTS: Fran, France, Frances, Frankie

Frayda

From the Yiddish word for 'joy'.
VARIANTS: Frayde, Fraydyne, Freida

Frederica

Of Old French and German origin, this name is made from the elements 'fred' ('peace') and 'ric' ('power, ruler').
VARIANTS: Federica, Fredda, Freddi, Freddie, Rica, Ricki

Freya

In Norse mythology, Freya was the goddess of fertility, love and beauty. The name means 'noble lady' or 'mistress'.
VARIANTS: Freja, Freyja, Froja

Gabrielle

Feminine form of Gabriel, from the Hebrew meaning 'messenger of God' or 'my strength is God'.
VARIANTS: Gabbie, Gabi, Gabriella, Gaby, Gaye, Gigi

Gaia

In Greek mythology Gaia was the goddess of the earth.
VARIANTS: Gaea, Ge

Gayle

A short form of the biblical name Abigail, from the Hebrew for 'my father rejoices' and 'source of joy'.
VARIANTS: Abigail, Abigayle, Gail, Gale

Gaynor

A diminutive of Guinevere, who was King Arthur's queen and Sir Lancelot's lover. It comes from the Welsh for 'beautiful maiden'.
VARIANTS: Gae, Gainer, Gay, Gayner

Gemma

Derived from the Latin for 'precious stone' or 'gem'.
VARIANTS: Gem, Germaine, Jemma

Geneviève

A French name from the German for 'womankind'.
VARIANTS: Geneva, Genevieve, Genny, Genovera, Genoveva, Gina

Georgette

A feminine version of George, which means 'farmer'.
VARIANTS: Georgett, Georgi, Georgia, Georgie, Gigi

Georgia

A feminine form of George, but also a place name in the USA, after King George.
VARIANTS: Georgett, Georgette, Georgi, Georgiana, Georgie, Georgina, Gigi

Geraldine

A romantic name coined by the 16th century writer Henry Howard. 'Gerald' is derived from a Germanic name that means 'spear' and 'rule'.
VARIANTS: Deena, Dina, Geralda, Geraldene, Geraldina, Gerrie

Germaine

From the Old French for 'German' and from the Latin for 'brother'.
VARIANTS: Gem, Gemma, Germain, Germana, Germane, Jermaine, Jermayn

Gigi

A French diminutive of Gilberte ('bright' and 'pledge') and Giselle ('pledge' and 'hostage').
VARIANTS: Gilbert, Giselle

Gila

From the Hebrew for 'joy'.
VARIANT: Ghila

Gilda

Thought to have been derived from the Old English for 'to gild' or 'to gloss over'.
VARIANTS: Gilde, Gildi, Gill, Jill

Gillian

The English form of Juliana, from the Greek for 'soft-haired' or 'fair-complexioned'.
VARIANTS: Gill, Gillaine, Gilly, Jill, Jillian, Jilly, Juliana

Gina

Originated as a pet form of the names Georgina ('farmer'), Eugena ('well-born, fortunate') and Regina ('queen').
VARIANTS: Eugena, Geena, Gena, Georgina, Jeanna, Regina

Ginger

A nickname for someone with red hair, as well as a pet form of Virginia.
VARIANT: Virginia

Giselle

From the German word for 'pledge'.
VARIANTS: Ghislaine, Gigi, Gisela, Giselda, Gisèle

Gita

As the short form of the Spanish Margarita, Gita means 'pearl' or 'daisy'. It could also stem from the Sanskrit for 'song'.
VARIANTS: Ghita, Greta, Gretchen, Gretel, Margaret, Margarita, Rita

Gloria

From the Latin for 'fame, renown, praise' and 'honour'.
VARIANTS: Glora, Gloriana, Glorianna, Glory

Goldie

A nickname for someone with blonde or fair hair.
VARIANTS: Golda, Goldia, Goldina

Grace

From the Latin 'gratus', which means 'pleasing', 'attractive' and 'charming'.
VARIANTS: Gracia, Gracie, Gráinne, Grata, Grayce, Grazielle

Greta

A short form of Margarita, from the Greek for 'pearl', or the French Marguerite, meaning 'daisy'.
VARIANTS: Daisy, Ghita, Gita, Gretchen, Gretel, Maggie, Margaret, Margarita, Marguerite, Rita

Gretchen

A German derivative of Margaret.
VARIANTS: Ghita, Gita, Greta, Gretel, Margaret, Margarita, Marguerite, Rita

Gwendolyn

A name from Arthurian legend, made up of the Welsh for 'white, fair' and 'ring or bow'.
VARIANTS: Gwen, Gwenda, Gwendelon, Gwendolina,

Gwenllian

From the Welsh meaning 'white flood' or 'fair flow'.
VARIANTS: Gwen, Gwenlian

Gwyneth

From the Celtic for 'blessed' or 'happy'.
VARIANTS: Gwen, Gwenda, Gwenith, Gwenn, Venetia, Wendi, Winnie

Habiba
From the Arabic for 'lover' and 'beloved'.
VARIANT: Haviva

Haidee
A variant of the Greek name Haido, which means 'to caress'. Also a variant of Heidi, which is a Swiss pet form of the German name Adelaide ('noble').
VARIANT: Heidi

Halina
From the Hawaiian for 'likeness' or 'resemblance'.

Halle
A variant of Hayley, meaning 'hay field' in Old English. Also thought to come from the Irish Gaelic for 'ingenious' and the Norse for 'hero'.
VARIANT: Hayley

Hana
Of Arabic origin, meaning 'bliss' or 'happiness'. It also means 'flower' or 'blossom' in Japanese, and 'sky' or 'dark cloud' in the Arapaho culture.
VARIANTS: Hanae, Hanako

Hannah
From the Hebrew for 'God has favoured me'.
VARIANTS: Ann, Anna, Annabel, Anne, Annette, Anoushka, Nanette

Harmony
In Greek mythology, Harmonia was the daughter of Aphrodite, the goddess of sex, love and beauty. Her name means 'agreement'.
VARIANTS: Harmonee, Harmoni, Harmonia, Harmonie

Harper
Originally an occupational surname for someone who played the harp.

Harriett
Feminine form of Harry, from Henry, meaning 'home rule'.
VARIANTS: Harrie, Harriet, Hat, Hattie, Henrietta, Hetta

Hayley
From the Old English for 'hay field'.
VARIANTS: Hailey, Haleigh, Haley, Hali, Halle, Hallie

Hazel
From the Old English word for 'hazelnut', and a colour associated with eyes.
VARIANTS: Hasse, Hazelle

Heather
A Scottish name and a wild plant with the Latin name Erica.

Hebe
In Greek mythology Hebe was the goddess of youth. It also the name of a flowering shrub.

Hedda
Derived from the German for 'combat' or 'war'.
VARIANT: Hedy

Heidi
A German form of the name Hilde, a variant of the English Hilda ('battle').
VARIANTS: Adelaide, Adeleid, Heide, Heidie, Hilde

Helen
From the Greek for 'ray', 'bright' and 'light'.
VARIANTS: Elaine, Eleanor, Elena, Ellen, Helena, Helene, Lena, Leonora

Helianthe
From the Greek for 'bright flower'.

Heloise

Thought to be of French origin, meaning 'famous fighter'.
VARIANTS: Eloisa, Eloïse, Eloise

Henrietta

The feminine form of the Germanic Henry, which means 'home rule'.
VARIANTS: Enrica, Harrie, Harriet, Harriett, Hat, Hattie, Henni

Hermione

A feminine form of Hermes, the messenger god who protected travellers, and whose name means 'stone' or 'support'.
VARIANTS: Erma, Hermia, Hermina, Hermine, Herminia, Mina

Hester

A variant of the biblical name Esther, from the Hebrew for 'bride'.
VARIANTS: Esther, Hettie, Hetty

Heulwen

This Welsh girl's name means 'sunshine'.

Hilary

Originally a boys' name, Hilary comes from the Greek 'hilaros', which means 'jovial', 'lively', 'cheerful' and 'boisterous'.
VARIANTS: Hilarie, Hillary

Holly

A name commonly bestowed on Christmas babies, from the Old English word 'holen', which means 'holly tree'.
VARIANTS: Holli, Hollie, Hollye

Honesty

A virtuous name of Latin origin.

Honey

A name that implies sweetness, from the Germanic 'honig'.

Honor

A Roman name for someone who commanded respect and recognition.
VARIANTS: Honora, Honoria, Honour

Hope

One of the three Christian virtues, from the Old English word 'hopa', meaning 'to desire or wish something to happen'.
VARIANTS: Hopi, Hopie

Hortense

Widely used in France, the name Hortense comes from the Latin for 'garden' or 'gardener'.
VARIANTS: Hortensia, Ortense, Ortensia

Hoshi

A Japanese name meaning 'star'.
VARIANTS: Hoshie, Hoshiko, Hoshiyo

Hula

From the Hebrew for 'to make music'.

Ida
Still popular in Scandinavia, from the Old Norse words for 'work' and 'woman'.
VARIANTS: Idane, Idina, Ita

Ilona
The Hungarian version of Helen, which means 'bright'.
VARIANTS: Eleanor, Helen, Helena, Ili, Ilonka, Lanci

Iman
Of African and Arabic origin, it means 'faith in God'.

Imelda
From the Latin for 'wishful', and also the Italian form of the Germanic name Irmhild, which means 'universal battle'.

Imogen
Possibly from the Latin word 'imago' ('image, likeness') or it could mean 'innocent', and it is also believed to be a misprint of Innogen, a Celtic name that means 'girl' or 'daughter'.
VARIANTS: Emogene, Imagina, Immie, Immy, Imogene, Imogine, Innogen, Inogen

Ina
A variant of Agnes, from the Greek for 'pure' and 'chaste', and also a short form of names such as Christina and Georgina, which end in 'ina'.
VARIANTS: Agnes, Ena

India
The Sanskrit word for 'river'.

Inés
The Spanish form of Agnes, derived from the Greek for 'pure' and 'chaste'.
VARIANTS: Agnes, Ines, Inez

Inge
From Ing, the Norse god of fertility, peace and plenty, Inge means 'meadow'.
VARIANTS: Inga, Ingaberg, Inger, Ingrid

Ingrid
From the Old Norse meaning 'Ing's ride or steed' or 'beautiful under the protection of Ing'.
VARIANTS: Inga, Ingaberg, Inge, Inger

Inoke
A Hawaiian name meaning 'devoted'.

Iola
From the Greek for 'violet' and 'dawn cloud'.
VARIANTS: Ianthe, Iole, Yolanda, Yolande

Iona
The name of a Scottish island.
VARIANTS: Ione, Ionia

Iora
From the Latin for 'gold'.

Iris
From the Greek for 'messenger of light' or 'rainbow', Iris is the name of a flower.
VARIANTS: Irisa, Irisha, Irissa, Irita, Irys, Risa, Risha, Rissa

Irma
A pet form of several Germanic names, meaning 'whole' or 'universal'.
VARIANTS: Emma, Erma, Irmgrad, Irmina, Irmintrude

Isabel
The Spanish equivalent of Elizabeth, which means 'God's oath' in Hebrew.
VARIANTS: Bel, Bell, Bella, Ezabel, Isabella, Isabelle, Isbel, Isobel, Izzie, Izzy

Isha
A variant of Aisha, from the Arabic for 'prospering'.
VARIANT: Aisha

Isla
Pronounced 'eye-la', this Scottish name means 'swiftly' and 'flowing'.
VARIANT: Islay

Ismaela
From the Hebrew for 'God listens'.

Isra
A Turkish name which means 'freedom'.

Ivy
This name is derived from the woodland clinging plant.
VARIANTS: Iva, Ivi, Ivie

Jacqueline

The French feminine form of the biblical name James, which is a variant of Jacob ('follower', 'supplanter').
VARIANTS: Jacki, Jackie, Jacklyn, Jacquelyn, Jacquelynne, Jacquetta, Jacqui

Jade

A precious green stone that is used to make carvings and jewellery.
VARIANT: Jayde

Jaime

From the French 'j'aime', which means 'I like' or 'I love', and in some cases a feminine form of James.
VARIANTS: Jaimi, Jaimie, Jamie, Jaymee

Jamelia

In Arabic this name means 'beautiful'.
VARIANTS: Djamila, Jameela, Jameelah, Jamilah, Jamillah, Jamillia

Jane

A feminine form of John, from the Hebrew for 'God has favoured' and 'God is gracious', and also derived from the Old French name Jehane.
VARIANTS: Janelle, Janet, Janette, Janice, Janie, Janine, Janis, Jayne, Jean, Joan

Janet

Another feminine derivation of John, via the French Jeanette.
VARIANTS: Janette, Janice, Janie, Janine, Janis, Jeanete, Jeannette, Jennie, Netta, Nettie, Jessie

Jasmine

A fragrant flower used to make tea, scented oil and perfume.
VARIANTS: Jasmin, Yasmin, Yasmina, Yasmine

Jean

A feminine variant of John, meaning 'God is gracious'.
VARIANTS: Gene, Genna, Jane, Janina, Janine, Jeanette, Jeanine, Jeanne, Jeannette, Jeannine

Jeanette

Diminutive form of Jean, from the biblical John, meaning 'God is gracious'.
VARIANT: Genette

Jemima

An Old Testament name which means 'dove'.
VARIANTS: Jem, Jemina, Jemimah, Jemma, Jona, Jonati, Mima

Jennifer

The Cornish version of Guinevere, which means 'fair ghost'.
VARIANTS: Gaenor, Gaynor, Guinevere, Jen, Jenna, Jenni, Jennie, Jenny

Jessica

Believed to be a Shakespearian creation as a feminine form of the biblical name Jesse, meaning 'riches' or 'a gift'.
VARIANTS: Jess, Jessie

Jewel

The word jewel comes from the Old French for 'plaything'.
VARIANTS: Jewell, Jewelle

Jill

From the ancient Roman clan of the Julii, whose name came from the Greek for 'fair skinned'.
VARIANTS: Gill, Gillian, Julia, Juliana, Julie

Joan

A French feminine form of John ('God is gracious').
VARIANTS: Jane, Janet, Jayne, Jean, Jeanne, Jo, Joanna, Joanne, Johanna

Joanne

A derivative of the French Joan, and also a combination of the names Jo and Anne.
VARIANTS: Giovanna, Jane, Janis, Jayne, Jean, Jeanne, Joan, Joann, Joanna, Johanna

Jocelin

From the Latin for 'sportive' or 'just', or from the Old German for 'descendant of the Goths'. Also, like Jacqueline, a German feminine form of Jacob ('follower', 'supplanter').
VARIANTS: Jocelyn, Josceline, Josette, Josie, Joss

Jodi

A short form of the biblical Judith ('Jewish woman'), and an elaboration of the pet name Jo.
VARIANTS: Jo, Joan, Joanne, Jodie, Jody, Josephine, Judi, Judith

Joleen

A feminine form of the biblical name Joseph, which means 'God will increase'.
VARIANTS: Jolene, Jolie, Joline, Josepha, Josephine

Jolie

From the French for 'pretty one' and the Middle English for 'jolly' or 'high-spirited'.
VARIANTS: Joleen, Jolene, Joli, Jolly

Jordan

Jordan is the name of a country and a river in the Middle East, which means 'flowing down'.
VARIANTS: Jordin, Jordyn, Jourdan

Josephine

Feminine form of the Biblical name Joseph, from the Hebrew 'God will increase'.
VARIANTS: Fifi, Jo, Jojo, Josey, Josefina, Josephina, Josie

Joss

A short form of the name Jocelin. The Celtic word 'josse' means 'champion'.
VARIANTS: Jacqueline, Jocelin, Jocelyn, Josse

Joy

Derived from the Old French word 'joie', meaning 'happiness'.
VARIANTS: Joi, Joyce, Joye

Joyce

A popular Irish surname, possibly derived from the Breton for 'Lord', or it could be a variant of Joy.
VARIANTS: Joice, Jossi, Jossie, Jossy, Joy

Julia

A derivation of the Roman family name Julius, which means 'fair-skinned'.
VARIANTS: Gill, Gillian, Gillie, Jill, Jillian, Juliana, Julie, Juliet

Julie

A French form of Julia.
VARIANTS: Gill, Gillian, Gillie, Jill, Jillian, Julia, Julie, Juliet

Juliet

Another derivation of the Roman name Julius, meaning 'fair-skinned'.
VARIANTS: Guiletta, Giulletta, Jules, Julia, Juliana, Juliette

June

From the month and the Roman supreme goddess Juno who gave it its name. June also comes from the Latin for 'young'.
VARIANTS: Juno, Una

Justine

A feminine form of Justin, which comes from the Latin for 'just, fair'.
VARIANT: Justina

Kalila
From the Arabic for 'beloved' and 'sweetheart'.

Kamala
An appellation of Lakshmi, the Hindu god of wealth, the name means 'lotus'.

Kamila
From the Arabic for 'complete', 'perfect' and 'perfect one'.
VARIANT: Kamilah

Kanani
In Hawaiian the name Kanani means 'beautiful'.
VARIANTS: Ani, Nani

Kara
A variant of the Italian Cara, which means 'beloved, dear'. 'Cara' is also the Irish Gaelic word for 'friend'.
VARIANT: Cara

Karen
The Scandinavian form of Catherine, which comes from the Greek for 'pure'.
VARIANTS: Caren, Caron, Caryn, Catherine, Karan, Kari, Karin, Karina, Karyn, Katherine

Karima
From 'karam', the Arabic for 'noble' and 'generous'.
VARIANTS: Kareema, Karimah, Kharim

Karis
Derived from the Greek for 'graceful'.

Karla
The feminine form of Karl, stemming from the Germanic Charles, which means 'man'.
VARIANTS: Carla, Carol, Caroline, Carrie, Kari, Karleen, Karlene, Karol, Karoline

Katarina
The Swedish form of Katherine ('pure').
VARIANTS: Catherine, Katerina, Katharina, Katherine

Kate
A short form of Katherine and Katarina.
VARIANTS: Catherine, Katarina, Kate, Katerina, Katharine, Katie, Katy

Katherine
Derived from the Greek word 'katharos', which means 'pure'.
VARIANTS: Catharine, Catherine, Karen, Katarina, Katerina, Katharine, Katherine, Kathlyn, Kathryn, Katie

Kay
A short form for names beginning with the letter 'K', but also a name derived from the Middle Low German for 'spear' or the Old English for 'key'.
VARIANTS: Kai, Kaye, Kayla, Kaylee, Kaylynn

Kayla
An elaboration of the name Kay and a variant of Kayleigh.
VARIANTS: Kay, Kaylah, Kayleigh, Kayley

Kayley
A transferred use of the Irish surname Kayleigh, which in Gaelic appears as Ó Caollaidhe ('descendant of Caollaidhe').
VARIANTS: Caileigh, Kailey, Kay, Kaylee, Kayleigh, Kayly

Keeleigh

From the Irish Gaelic for 'beautiful girl', and is also rooted in the word 'cadhla', which means 'graceful'.
VARIANTS: Kayleigh, Kayley, Keelie, Keely, Keighley, Kelly

Keira

From the Irish word for black, 'ciar', the name means 'little dark one' or 'dark-haired'.
VARIANTS: Ciara, Ciaragh, Kiara, Kiera

Keisha

Possibly derived from the word 'nkisa', meaning 'favourite' in the African Bobangi language, or a modern blending of the name Aisha with the letter 'K'.
VARIANTS: Aisha, Keesha, Kiesha, LaKeisha

Kelila

A Hebrew name which means 'crowned with laurel'. Also a feminine form of Kyle.
VARIANTS: Kaila, Kaile, Kayle, Kelilah, Kelula, Kyla, Kylene

Kelly

From the Irish surname Ó Cellaigh, which means 'descendant of Ceallach'.
VARIANTS: Kaley, Keeleigh, Keeley, Keli, Kellee, Kelli

Kendra

Thought to stem from the Old English word for 'knowledge', it could also be a blend of the male and female names Ken and Sandra.
VARIANTS: Ken, Kendis

Kenya

The name of a country, now quite popular as a girl's name.

Keren

A short form of the biblical Kerenhappuch, which comes from the Hebrew for 'animal horn' or 'horn of eye-shadow'. The name refers to the material from which boxes, which contained kohl to decorate the eyes, were made.
VARIANTS: Kaaren, Kareen, Karen, Karin, Karon, Karyn, Kerryn, Kyran

Kerry

The name of an Irish county, derived from 'ciar', a Gaelic word meaning 'dark one'.
VARIANTS: Ceri, Keree, Keri, Kerrey

Keshisha

Derived from the Aramaic for 'elder'.

Ketifa

An Arabic name meaning 'to pluck a flower'.

Keziah

A biblical name from the Hebrew for 'cassia', a type of fragrant shrub.
VARIANTS: Kasia, Kerzia, Kesia, Kesiah, Ketzi, Ketzia, Kez, Kizzie

Kiara

A feminine form of the Celtic name Kieran, which means 'dark one' or 'dark-haired'. Also a variant of Chiara, the Italian form of Clare, which means 'bright' and 'clear'.
VARIANTS: Chiara, Ciara, Clare, Keira, Kiera

Kiki

A short form of names beginning with the letter 'K'. It is also derived from an African name meaning 'funny girl'.

Kimberly

A town in South Africa where British troops were stationed during the Boer War, and also the site of a famous diamond mine.
VARIANTS: Kim, Kimberlee, Kimberley, Kimberlie, Kimmi, Kimmie, Kym

Kimi

A Japanese name meaning 'sovereign', 'best' and 'without equal'.
VARIANTS: Kimie, Kimiko, Kimiyo

Kira

A Persian name that means 'sun', 'throne' and 'shepherd', and a variant spelling of Keira.
VARIANTS: Ciara, Keira, Kiara, Kiera

Kirsten

A Scandinavian variant of Christine, meaning 'Christian' or 'follower of Christ'. Also derived from the Old English for 'church' and the Greek for 'of the Lord'.
VARIANTS: Christine, Kersten, Kiersten, Kirby, Kirstie, Kirsty

Koko

A Japanese name which symbolises longevity. It means 'stork'.

Kristen

A Scandinavian form of Christine, which means 'Christian'.
VARIANTS: Christine, Kirsten, Krista, Kristeen, Kristina, Krysta, Krystina

Kylie

A popular Australian name derived from an Aboriginal word that means 'boomerang'.
VARIANTS: Kylee, Kyleigh, Kyley

Kyna

From the Irish Gaelic for 'wisdom' and 'intelligence'.

Laila

A name of Arabic origin, meaning 'night', 'dark-haired' or 'dark-skinned'.
VARIANTS: Laili, Laleh, Layla, Leala, Lee, Leigh, Leila, Leyla, Lila, Lilah

Lakshmi

The Hindu goddess of wealth, beauty, fertility and luck, from the Sanskrit for 'mark' or 'birthmark'.

Lalita

An Indian term of endearment from the Sanskrit for 'charming', 'honest' and 'straightforward'.
VARIANTS: Lal, Lalie, Lita

Lana

A short form of Alana, the feminine version of Alan, believed to be derived from the Celtic for 'harmony', or from 'Alannah', from the Irish Gaelic meaning 'o child'. Other possible sources are the Latin word 'lanatus', which means 'woolly' or 'downy', the Hawaiian word for 'buoyant' and the Breton for 'rock'.
VARIANTS: Alana, Alanah, Alanna, Alannah, Lane, Lanette, Lanna, Lanne, Lannie, Lanny

Lara

A name from Roman mythology and also a short form of Larissa.
VARIANTS: Larissa, Laura

Larissa

Larissa appears in Greek mythology and is now the name of a moon and an asteroid.
VARIANTS: Lara, Larisa, Laura

Lauren

A variant of Laura, which means 'laurel'.
VARIANTS: Lara, Larissa, Laura, Lauryn, Loraine, Loren

Lavender

A sweet-smelling plant with clusters of small, mauve flowers. The name is of Latin origin and means 'to wash'.

Lavern

From Laverna, the Roman goddess of thieves and conmen, whose name was the Latin for 'springtime'.
VARIANTS: Laverna, Laverne, La Verne, Luvern

Leah

A biblical name which means 'languid' or 'weary'.
VARIANTS: Lea, Lee, Leigh, Lia, Liah

Leigh

A variant of the English surname Lee, meaning 'meadow', a variant of the biblical Leah ('weary') and of the Arabic name Laila, meaning 'night' or 'dark complexion'.
VARIANTS: Laila, Leah, Lee, Leila

Leilani

A Hawaiian name meaning 'heavenly child' or 'heavenly flower'.
VARIANTS: Lei, Lelani

Leoma

From the Old English for 'light' and 'brightness'.

Leona

A feminine elaboration of Leo, which means 'lion' in Latin, and also a variant of the name Eleanor via Leonora.
VARIANTS: Eleanor, Helen, Leonie, Leonora

Lesley

From the Scottish Gaelic meaning 'low-lying meadow' and 'garden of hollies'.
VARIANTS: Lea, Lesli, Leslie, Lesly, Lezlie

Letifa

From the Arabic word 'latif', which means 'gentle'.
VARIANTS: Latifah, Letipha

Letitia

From the Latin for 'joyful' or 'unrestrained joy'.
VARIANTS: Laetitia, Lece, Lecia, Leta, Letisha, Lettice, Lettie, Tisha, Titia

Levanna

The Roman goddess of newborn babies, whose name comes from the Latin for 'lifting up' and 'rising sun'.
VARIANTS: Levana, Levona, Livana, Livona

Levina

From the Middle English for 'lightning'.

Lianne

A French variant of Juliana ('fair-skinned') and Elaine ('bright'), or a compound of Lee ('meadow') and Anne ('God has favoured me'), from English and Hebrew.
VARIANTS: Ann, Anne, Elaine, Helen, Leana, Leann, Leanne, Lee, Lianna

Liberty

From the Latin 'libertas', meaning 'freedom'.
VARIANTS: Lib, Libbie, Libby

Lilac

Both a colour and a plant, from the Persian and Arabic for 'indigo' and 'blue'.

Lillian

A variant of Elizabeth, meaning 'God is perfection', and also an elaboration of the flower name 'lily'.
VARIANTS: Elizabeth, Liliana, Lilibet, Lily, Lilly

Lily

Derived from the flower, a symbol of purity, and also a short form of Elizabeth.
VARIANTS: Elizabeth, Lilibet, Lilith, Lillian, Lilly

Lindsey

Originally a surname, which may stem from the Old English for a place name meaning 'wetland' or 'waterside linden trees'.
VARIANT: Lindsay

Linnea

From Linnaea, the national flower of Sweden.
VARIANTS: Linea, Linna, Linnae, Linnaea, Lynea, Lynnea

Lisa

Originally a pet form of Elizabeth ('God is perfection'), but now a variant of Liza, which is short for Eliza.
VARIANTS: Elisa, Elisabeth, Eliza, Elizabeth, Liza

Lois

A name from the New Testament, and also a contraction of the French names Heloise and Eloise.
VARIANTS: Eloise, Heloise, Louise

Lola

A name mostly found in Spanish-speaking countries as a short form of Dolores ('sorrows').
VARIANTS: Delores, Dolores, Lita, Lo, Lolita

Lolita

A pet form of Lolita, short for Dolores, meaning 'sorrow'.
VARIANTS: Delores, Dolores, Lita, Lo, Lola, Loleta

Lonnie

Derives from Leona, which means 'lion' or 'bright'.
VARIANTS: Eleanor, Elenora, Leona

Lorelei

The name of a huge rock on the River Rhine in Germany, which passed into legend as the home of a siren whose song lured sailors on to the rocks.
VARIANTS: Lorelie, Lorilee, Lura, Lurette, Lurleen, Lurlene, Lurline

Lorraine

From the French place name, Lorraine.
VARIANTS: Laraine, Lauraine, Loraine, Lori

Lotus

An exotic flower that is native to both Asia and Africa.

Louise

From the Frankish name Clodowig, via Clovis, which means 'famous battle'.
VARIANTS: Aloise, Eloise, Heloise, Louisa, Louisetta

Lourdes

A place in southern France, sacred to Roman Catholics for its supposedly healing waters.
VARIANT: Lola

Lowri

The Welsh form of Laura, which comes from the Latin for 'laurel'.
VARIANT: Laura

Lucinda

From the Latin 'lucere', which means 'to shine, glitter or be light'.
VARIANTS: Cindi, Cindy, Lucia, Lucy, Sindy

Lucy

A variant of Lucia, from the Latin for 'light' or 'bringer of light'.
VARIANTS: Luci, Lucia, Lucille, Lucinda

Lulie

From the Middle English word 'lullen', Lulie means to 'soothe', 'cause sleep' or 'dispel fears'.

Lulu

A pet form of Louise, meaning 'famed warrior' or 'famous battle', and Lucy, meaning 'light'.
VARIANTS: Leu, Lleulu, Louise, Lucy

Luna

The Roman goddess of the moon, whose name means 'moon' or 'crescent'.
VARIANT: Lunette

Lynne

From the Welsh Eluned, which means 'idol' or 'icon', or the Old English word 'hylynna', which means 'brook'. Also a short form of names ending in 'line', such as Caroline.
VARIANTS: Eiluned, Eluned, Lin, Linn, Lynn

Lys

From the medieval French for 'lily', as well as a short form of Elizabeth ('God is perfection').
VARIANTS: Elizabeth, Liz, Lizi, Lizzie

Lysandra

Feminine form of Lysander, from the Greek meaning 'freer of men'.
VARIANTS: Sandie, Sandra, Sandy

Mabel

A derivation of the Latin word 'amabilis', meaning 'worthy of love', which developed into Amabel and Amabella.
VARIANTS: Amabel, Amabella, Mab, Mabell, Mabella, Mabelle, Mable, May, Maybell, Maybelle

Macy

Originally a surname taken from a French place name.
VARIANTS: Macey, Maci, Macie

Madeline

A French variant of the biblical Magdalene, which meant 'from Magdala'.
VARIANTS: Madalain, Madaline, Madaliene, Madeleine, Magda, Magdalen, Magdalene,

Madison

Originally a surname meaning 'Matthew's son', 'Maud's son' or 'Madde's son'.
VARIANTS: Maddie, Maddison, Maddy

Madra

From the Spanish for 'mother'.
VARIANT: Madre

Maeve

Derived from 'meadhbh', an Irish Celtic warrior queen, whose name meant 'intoxicating' or 'joy'.
VARIANTS: Meave, Meaveen

Magdalene

A biblical name meaning 'from Magdala', a village by the Sea of Galilee. Sometimes pronounced 'Maud-lin'.
VARIANTS: Madalena, Madelena, Madeleine, Madeline, Magdalen, Magdalena, Maude, Maudlin

Mahira

From the Hebrew and Italian for 'energetic' and 'quick', and also from the Arabic for 'young' and 'horse'.
VARIANT: Mehira

Maia

A character from Greek mythology whose name means 'nurse' or 'mother'. Also a Roman goddess who gave her name to the month of May.
VARIANTS: Mae, Mai, May, Maya

Mairin

The Irish form of Mary, which means 'dew of the sea'.
VARIANTS: Mary, Maureen

Maisie

Scottish variant of Margaret.
VARIANT: Maisy

Majesta

From the Latin for 'greatness' and 'grandeur'.

Makani

A Hawaiian name that means 'wind'.

Malu

Short for Malulani, a Hawaiian name that means 'beneath peaceful skies'.
VARIANT: Malulani

Manuela

A Spanish name derived from the biblical Emmanuel, which means 'God is with us'.
VARIANTS: Emanuella, Emmanuela

Marcella

The feminine form of Marcel, derived from Mars, the god of war.
VARIANTS: Marcela, Marcelle, Marcellina, Marcelyn, Marcille

Mardell
From the Old English for 'meadow near the sea'.

Margaret
From the Latin for 'pearl', though the French form Marguerite means 'daisy' because that flower is associated with a saint bearing the name.
VARIANTS: Greta, Maggie, Majorie, Margarita, Margaux, Margherita, Margot, Marguerite, Meg, Rita

Margot
A pet form of the French Marguerite, pronounced 'Margo'.
VARIANTS: Margaret, Margaux, Margo, Marguerite

Marigold
A yellow and orange flower whose name comes from the Old English for 'Mary's gold', in reference to the Virgin Mary.
VARIANTS: Goldie, Goldy, Mari, Marie, Mary, Marygold

Maria
A variant of the biblical Mary, and also related to the earlier name Miriam, it comes from the Hebrew for 'longed for child' and 'rebellion'.
VARIANTS: Mariah, Mariam, Mary, Maryam, Miriam

Mariah
A variant of Maria, and also derived from the Latin for 'bitter' and 'God is my teacher'.
VARIANTS: Maria, Mariam, Mary, Maryam, Miriam

Marilyn
An elaboration of Mary in conjunction with the name Lyn.
VARIANTS: Lyn, Lynne, Mari, Marilynn, Mary, Marylyn, Marylynn

Marina
From the Latin 'marinus', meaning 'belonging to the sea' or 'produced by the sea'.
VARIANTS: Mare, Maren, Marena, Maris, Marissa, Marna, Marne, Rina

Marini
A Swahili name that means 'healthy', 'fresh' and 'pretty'.

Marissa
An elaboration of the biblical name Mary ('longed for child' and 'rebellion'), as well as coming from the Latin for 'of the sea'.
VARIANTS: Mareesa, Mari, Maria, Mariah, Marie, Marina, Marisa, Mary, Risa, Rissa

Marquita
A variant of Marketa and Marcella, derived from the Roman god Mars.
VARIANT: Marquite

Martha
A New Testament name which comes from the Aramaic for 'lady'.
VARIANTS: Mardi, Marta, Marthe, Martie, Mat, Mattie, Matty, Pattie, Patty

Marva
From the Hebrew word for the fragrant herb, 'sage'.

Mary

One of the most popular biblical names of all time, in the Old Testament the name appears as Miriam and comes from the Hebrew for 'sea of bitterness' or 'longed-for child'.

VARIANTS: Maria, Mariah, Marianne, Marie, Marilyn, Marissa, Marylou, Maryam, Maureen, Moira, Molly

Marylou

A combination of Mary ('longed-for child') and Louise ('famed battle').

VARIANTS: Lou, Louise, Marie, Marilou, Mary, Miriam

Matilda

A Norman name from two words meaning 'might' and 'battle'.

VARIANTS: Matelda, Mathilda, Matildis, Matti, Maud, Maude, Maudie, Mawde, Tilda, Tillie

May

Taken from the month, named after the Roman goddess Maia, and also a short form of Mary and Margaret.

VARIANTS: Mae, Mai, Maia, Margaret, Mary, Maya, Maybelle, Mei

Mavis

From the Old French 'mauvis', which means 'song thrush'.

VARIANTS: Maeve, Mave

Meera

An Indian name meaning 'saintly woman', and a Hebrew name meaning 'radiant' and 'light'.

Megan

The Welsh elaboration of Meg, which is a pet form of Margaret.

VARIANTS: Maegan, Maygen, Meag(h)an

Melanie

Derived from the Greek mythological character Melanion, whose name meant 'black' or 'dark complexion'.

VARIANTS: Melany, Melony

Mercy

The virtue of 'compassionate' and 'pity'.

VARIANTS: Mercedes, Merica, Mercille, Merry

Merit

From the Latin word 'meritus', which means 'earned' and 'deserved'.

VARIANT: Merritt

Merle

From the Latin for 'blackbird', and also a variant of Muriel, from the Irish Gaelic for 'sea' and 'bright'.

VARIANTS: Merla, Merlene, Merlina, Muriel, Myrl, Myrle

Mia

An Italian name derived from the Latin for 'mine'. Can be pronounced 'Me-ah' or as 'My-ah'.

Michaela

Feminine form of Michael, from the Hebrew for 'who is like God'.

VARIANTS: Mica, Michael, Michaelle, Michelle, Miia, Mikelina

Michelle

Feminine form of Michael, from the Hebrew for 'who is like God'.
VARIANTS: Chelle, Michael, Michaela, Michaelle, Shell

Milly

A short form of a number of names, including Amelia ('toil'), Camilla ('one who helps at sacrifices'), Mildred ('gentle strength') and Millicent ('strong worker', 'determined'). Also from the Israeli for 'who is for me?'.
VARIANTS: Amelia, Camilla, Mildred, Millicent, Millie

Mina

From the Old German word for 'love', the Japanese for 'south' and the Persian for 'daisy'. Also a short form of the German name Wilhelmina, which means 'will' and 'protection'.
VARIANTS: Minella, Minna, Minnie, Wilhelmina, Willa, Wilma

Mirabel

From the Latin word 'mirabilis', which means 'marvellous'.
VARIANTS: Bella, Belle, Mira, Mirabella, Mirabelle, Mirella

Miranda

From the Latin for 'wonderful' and 'admirable'.
VARIANTS: Maranda, Marenda, Meranda, Mina, Mira, Mirabel, Mirinda, Myranda, Randi, Randy

Miriam

A biblical name that was an earlier form of Mary and means 'longed for child' and 'rebellion'.
VARIANTS: Maria, Marian, Marianne, Mary, Maryam, Meryem, Mimi, Minnie, Mitzi

Misty

From the Old English for 'clouded' and 'obscure'.
VARIANTS: Misti, Mistie, Mystee, Mysti, Mystie, Mystique

Moira

Anglicised form of Maire, the Irish version of Mary. In Greek mythology the Moirae were the Three Fates who were the embodiment of destiny.
VARIANTS: Maire, Mary, Maura, Maureen, Miriam, Moirae, Moreen, Moyra

Molly

From Mally, which was a pet form of Mary.
VARIANT: Mary

Mona

Immortalised by the Leonardo da Vinci painting 'Mona Lisa', the name has possible origins in Greek ('alone' or 'just'), Irish Gaelic (a combination of 'noble', 'nun' and 'angel'), Arabic ('wish'), Old English ('month') and Latin (for the Welsh island Anglesey). Also a short form of Monica.
VARIANTS: Madonna, Monica, Monique, Monna, Moyna, Muna

Monica

From the Latin meaning 'to warn' or 'advise'.
VARIANTS: Mona, Monique

Morag

An Irish Gaelic name which means 'great', 'sun' and 'young one'. Also the Scottish version of Sarah, which means 'princess' in Hebrew.
VARIANTS: Marion, Moirin, Moreen, Sarah

Morgan

Variant of Morgana, from Arthurian legend, whose name comes from the Welsh for 'sea' and 'bright' or 'great' and 'born'.
VARIANT: Morgana

Morwenna

From the Welsh 'morwyn', which means 'a maiden'.
VARIANTS: Maureen, Morwen, Morwyn, Wenna, Wennie, Wenny

Muriel

From the Irish words 'muir' ('sea') and 'geal' ('bright').
VARIANTS: Marial, Meriel, Merril, Merrill, Meryl, Muriell, Murielle

Myfanwy

A Welsh name meaning 'rare one' or 'my treasure'.
VARIANTS: Fanni, Fannie, Fanny, Myf, Myfi, Myfina

Myrna

An Arabic name derived from myrrh, the reddish-brown material used in perfumes and incense. Also a variant of the Irish name Muirne, which means 'blood'.
VARIANTS: Merna, Mirna, Morna, Muirna, Muirne

Naama

From the Hebrew for 'beautiful' and 'pleasant' and the Arabic for 'good fortune'.
VARIANTS: Naamah, Naava

Nadia

Pet form of the Russian name Nadezhda, which means 'hope'.
VARIANTS: Nada, Nadeen, Nadie, Nadina, Nadine, Nadja, Nadka

Naia

From the Greek Naiads, mythological water nymphs who were destined always to look young.
VARIANTS: Naiad, Naida, Naiia, Nalda

Nancy

Derived from the biblical name Hannah, meaning 'God has favoured me', via Anne, and also a variant of Agnes, from the Greek 'hagnos' meaning 'pure' or 'holy'.
VARIANTS: Agnes, Ann, Anna, Anne, Hannah, Nance, Nancie, Nanette

Nanette

The French version of Nancy as a pet form of Anne.
VARIANTS: Ann, Anna, Anne, Hannah, Nance, Nancie, Nancy, Nannie, Nanny

Naomi

A biblical name from the Hebrew for 'delightful', 'pleasant' and 'charming'.
VARIANTS: Nae, Naome, Noemi, Nomi

Natalie

From the Latin word 'natalis', which means 'birthday' and is traditionally associated with the birth of Christ ('nativity').
VARIANTS: Natalia, Natalya, Natasha, Natassia, Nathalie, Talia

Natasha

The feminine form of Nathan, from the Hebrew for 'gift', and also a Russian pet form of Natalie.
VARIANTS: Natacha, Natalia, Natalie, Natalya, Natasja, Natassia, Nathalie, Tasha

Nebula

From the Latin for 'mist', 'smoke' and 'darkness'.

Nell

Short form of Cornelia or Helen.
VARIANTS: Eleanor, Ellen, Nellie, Nelly

Nerissa

A character in Shakespeare's 'The Merchant of Venice', possibly derived from Nereus, a Greek god of the sea, whose daughters were called the Neireids.
VARIANTS: Nerida, Nerina

Nerys

From the Welsh word 'ner', which means 'lord'.

Ngaire

An Antipodean name from the Maori word 'ngaio', which means 'clever'.
VARIANT: Ngaio

Niamh

Pronounced 'Neeve', a goddess from Irish mythology whose name means 'bright'.
VARIANTS: Nia, Niar

Nicole

French feminine form of Nicholas, from the Greek for 'people's victory'.
VARIANTS: Nichole, Nicola, Nicolette, Nicci

Nikita

Originally a boy's name in Russia from the Greek for 'unconquered'. Also an Indian name that means 'the earth'.

Nissa

From the Hebrew meaning 'sign', 'emblem' or 'to test', and also comes from the African Hausa language for 'never-forgotten loved one'.
VARIANTS: Nissie, Nissy

Nokomis

A Native American name which means 'daughter of the moon'.

Nola

A feminine version of the Irish name Nolan, meaning 'son of the noble one', as well as a derivation of the Celtic Fionnuala, which means 'fair-shouldered'.
VARIANTS: Fiona, Fionnuala, Nolana, Noleen, Nolene, Nuala

Nona

From the Latin for ninth, a name traditionally bestowed on a ninth-born child in Victorian times, or a child born in September, the ninth month.
VARIANTS: Noni, Nonie

Norah

A short form of Eleanor, Leonora (both from Helen, meaning 'bright' or 'light') and Honoria ('honour'). Also a derivative of Nuala, from the Celtic Fionnuala ('fair-shouldered').
VARIANTS: Eleanor, Fionnuala, Helen, Honor, Honoria, Nora

Nova

From the Latin for 'new'.
VARIANT: Novia

Nuala

A popular Irish name derived from the Celtic Fionnuala ('fair-shouldered'). It is pronounced 'New-la'.
VARIANTS: Fenella, Fionnghuala, Fionnuala, Nola, Nora

Octavia

From the Latin for 'eight', traditionally given to the eighth child.
VARIANTS: Octavia, Octavio, Tave, Tavia, Tavy

Odessa

From the Greek 'odyssey', which means 'extended wandering' or 'epic voyage'.

Olga

A popular Russian name derived from an Old Norse adjective that means 'prosperous' and 'successful'.
VARIANTS: Helga, Ola, Olenka, Olia, Olina, Olli, Ollie

Olive

From the fruit and tree of the same name, which is associated with peace.
VARIANTS: Livvy, Olivia

Olivia

A variant of Olive, from the Latin 'oliva' for olive tree.
VARIANTS: Livia, Livvy, Oliva, Olive

Olwyn

From the Welsh meaning 'white footprint', Olwyn was a character from Celtic legend whose footprints were covered in white clover.
VARIANTS: Olwen, Olwin

Olympia

From the Greek 'Olympus', the seat of the gods.
VARIANTS: Olimpia, Olimpie, Olympias

Opal

From the Sanskrit 'upalas', meaning 'precious stone'.

Ophelia

A tragic character from Shakespeare's 'Hamlet', probably derived from the Greek word 'ophelos', which means 'help'.
VARIANTS: Ofelia, Ofilia, Ophelie

Orchid

An exotic flower, generally associated with luxury.

Orla

From the Irish for 'golden lady' or 'golden princess'.
VARIANTS: Orfhlaith, Orlagh

Paige
From the Old English 'page', for a young servant, which comes from the Greek for 'child'.
VARIANT: Page

Paloma
A Spanish name which means 'dove'.
VARIANTS: Palloma, Palometa, Palomita, Peloma

Pamela
An invention of the 16th century English poet Sir Philip Sidney, believed to be a combination of the Greek words 'pau' ('all') and 'meli' ('honey').
VARIANTS: Pam, Pamelia, Pamelina, Pamella, Pammi, Pammy

Pandora
In Greek mythology, Pandora was the first woman, created by Zeus for the confusion of men, and her name means 'all gifts'.
VARIANT: Panda

Paris
The French capital, named after the Celtic tribe the Parisii, but also the name of the Trojan prince who abducted Helen and sparked the Trojan War.

Patience
A Christian virtue, from the Latin word 'pati', which means 'to suffer' or 'endure'.
VARIANTS: Pat, Pattie, Patty

Patricia
The feminine form of Patrick, from the Latin for 'noble one'.
VARIANTS: Pat, Patrice, Patrizia, Patsy, Pattie, Patty, Rickie, Ricky, Tish, Tricia, Trish

Paula
A saint's name, the feminine form of Paul, from the Latin for 'small'.
VARIANTS: Paola, Pauletta, Paulette, Paulina, Pauline, Paulita

Pearl
Sometimes used as a pet form of Margaret, as the Greek for 'pearl' is 'margaretes'. The variant Perle is an Anglicised version of the Yiddish Penninah, which means 'coral'.
VARIANTS: Margaret, Pearlie, Pearline, Peninnah, Pennina, Perla, Perle

Penelope
A name made famous by Homer's 'Odyssey', Penelope means 'weaver'.
VARIANTS: Penelopa, Pennie, Penny, Popi

Peta
A Scandinavian feminine version of Peter, from the Greek for 'stone'.
VARIANT: Pet, Petra

Petra
From the Latin and Greek for 'stone'.
VARIANTS: Pet, Peta, Petie

Petula
Thought to come from the Latin for 'forward', 'saucy' and 'impudent', or possibly from the Latin word 'petulare' meaning 'to ask'.
VARIANT: Pet

Philippa
Feminine form of the biblical name Philip, which means 'horse lover'.
VARIANTS: Felipa, Filipa, Phillipa, Philly, Pip, Pippa

Phoebe

The alternative name for Artemis, the goddess of the moon, from the Greek and Latin for 'bright' and 'shining'.
VARIANT: Phebe

Phoenix

This sacred bird from Egyptian mythology takes its name from the Greek word 'phyllidis', which means 'leafy branch'.
VARIANTS: Phillis, Phylis, Phyllida, Phyllis

Poppy

A symbolic flower whose name comes from the Old English 'popaeg'.
VARIANTS: Poppi, Poppie

Portia

A name used by Shakespeare in 'Julius Caesar' and 'The Merchant of Venice', derived from the Roman family name Porcius, from the Latin for 'pig'.
VARIANTS: Porchia, Porsche, Porsha, Porshia

Precious

A name that means 'priceless' and 'treasured'.

Primrose

A pale-yellow spring flower that derives its name from the Latin 'prima rosa', meaning 'first rose'.
VARIANT: Rose

Priscilla

A biblical name from the Latin for 'ancient', 'old-fashioned' and 'antique'.
VARIANTS: Cilla, Precilla, Prescilla, Pricilla, Pris, Prissy, Silla

Quinn

Associated with the Latin word for 'fifth', and also a variant of Queenie, from the Old English and Old Norse for 'wife', 'companion' and 'woman'.
VARIANTS: Queenie, Quinta, Quintana, Quintilla, Quintina

Rachel

A biblical name from the Hebrew for 'ewe'.
VARIANTS: Rachael, Rachele, Racheli, Raquel, Ray, Raye, Rochell, Shell, Shelley

Raquel

The Spanish form of Rachel, from the Hebrew for 'ewe'.
VARIANTS: Rachael, Rachel, Rachelle, Raquelle

Rashida

In Sanskrit and Arabic, Rashida means 'follower of the correct path'.
VARIANTS: Rasheeda, Rashi

Rebecca

An Old Testament name taken from the Hebrew and Aramaic 'ribkah', which means 'knotted cord' and implies a faithful wife.
VARIANTS: Bec, Becca, Beck, Beckie, Becky, Bekky, Bex, Reba, Rebe, Rebekah

Reese

A feminine variant of the Welsh boys' name Rhys, which means 'ardour' or 'rashness'.
VARIANTS: Reece, Rees

Rhea

The mother of Zeus in Greek mythology, her name means 'flowing' or 'protector'.
VARIANTS: Rea, Reanna, Ria

Ria

From the Spanish for 'small river' or 'river mouth'. Also a variant of Rhea ('flowing' or 'protector') and a pet form of names ending in 'ria', such as Maria.
VARIANTS: Maria, Rhea, Victoria

Rita

A short form of Margarita, and also derived from Hindi meaning 'brave', 'strong' or 'proper'.
VARIANTS: Daisy, Margaret, Margarita, Margherita, Marguerita, Marguerite, Reda, Reeta, Reida

Robyn

The feminine form of Robin, which is a pet form of Robert ('fame' and 'bright'), as well as a reference to the bird.

Rose

A reference to the flower associated with romance, or possibly derived from Germanic words for 'horse' and 'fame'.
VARIANTS: Rosa, Rosabella, Rosalie, Rosalind, Rosanna, Rosanne, Rosemary, Rosetta, Rosie, Rosina, Rosita

Roxanne

Thought to come from the Persian word for 'dawn'.
VARIANTS: Roxana, Roxane, Roxy

Ruby

A red gemstone, from the Latin 'rubeus', meaning red.
VARIANTS: Rubetta, Rubette, Rubi, Rubia, Rubina

Ruth

An Old Testament name associated with companionship and friendship.
VARIANT: Ruthie

Sabrina

The Celtic name for the River Severn in England, supposedly derived from the illegitimate daughter of a Welsh king.

VARIANT: Zabrina

Saffron

A rare and exotic spice produced from the crocus flower, from the Arabic word 'zafaron', which means 'crocus'.

VARIANTS: Saffie, Safflower, Saffrey, Saffy

Sage

The name of a herb and also a word that means 'wise'.

Sahara

From the African desert, whose name is from the Arabic 'sahra'.

VARIANT: Zahara

Salena

From the Latin word 'sal', meaning 'salt' and 'salt water'.

VARIANT: Salina

Sally

Originally a pet form of Sarah, a Hebrew name meaning 'princess'.

VARIANTS: Sal, Sallie, Sally-Ann, Sarah

Salome

A biblical name from the Hebrew 'shalom', meaning 'peace'.

VARIANTS: Sal, Salama, Salomi, Saolma, Shulamit

Samantha

Possibly the feminine equivalent of the biblical Samuel, from the Hebrew for 'heard by God', or from the Aramaic for 'one who listens'.

VARIANTS: Sam, Sammie, Sammy

Samira

From the Arabic for 'entertainer' and 'companion in night talk'.

VARIANTS: Mira, Sam, Sami, Sammie, Sammy

Sarah

An Old Testament name meaning 'princess'.

VARIANTS: Morag, Sara, Sarai, Saran, Sarann

Saskia

Thought to stem from the Germanic word 'Sachs', which means 'Saxon'.

Selma

From the Celtic meaning 'fair', and also from the Old Norse for 'divinely protected'.

VARIANTS: Aselma, Zelma

Shannon

The name of the longest river in Ireland, Shannon means 'descendant of Sean' in Gaelic.

VARIANTS: Shanna, Shannagh

Siân

The Celtic version of Jane, which is a feminine form of John ('God is gracious').

VARIANTS: Jane, Janet, Jayne, Jeanette, Sian, Siani, Shani

Sierra
From the Spanish for 'saw', also used to denote a 'mountain range'.

Sinéad
The Gaelic version of Jane and Janet, both of which are derived from John ('God is gracious'). Pronounced 'Shin-aid' or 'Sin-aid'.
VARIANTS: Jane, Janet, Jayne, Jeanette, Sinead

Skye
A short form of the Dutch name Skyler, meaning 'fugitive', a reference to the Scottish island or a variant of the nature name Sky.
VARIANT: Sky

Sophie
A variant of the Greek 'Sophia', which means 'wisdom'.
VARIANTS: Sofi, Sofia, Sofya, Sonia, Sondya, Sonja, Sonni, Sophia

Stella
From the Latin for 'star'.

Susan
A short form of the biblical Susannah, whose name comes from the Hebrew word 'shoshana' meaning 'lily'.
VARIANTS: Chana, Shoshan, Siusan, Suki, Susana, Susannah, Susanne, Suzannah, Suzanne

Tabitha

A biblical name from the Aramaic for 'gazelle'.
VARIANTS: Tab, Tabatha, Tabbi, Tabbie, Tabbitha, Tabby

Tali

A short form of the biblical Talitha, meaning 'little girl' or 'little lamb', or of Tallulah, from the Native American Indian meaning 'leaping water'.
VARIANTS: Tal, Talitha, Tallulah, Tally

Tamara

From the Arabic and Hebrew for 'date palm tree'.
VARIANTS: Mara, Tam, Tamah, Tamar, Tamarah, Tammi, Tammy, Timi

Tammy

A pet form of Tamara and Tamsin.
VARIANTS: Tami, Tammi, Tammie

Tamsin

A feminine version of the biblical Thomas, from the Arabic for 'twin'.
VARIANTS: Tamasin, Tamasine, Tami, Tammie, Tammy, Tamzin, Thomasina, Thomasine

Tania

Short for the Russian Tatiana and the Greek Titania, which means 'giant'.
VARIANTS: Tanya, Tatiana, Tita, Titania

Tara

The name of a hill in Ireland, which was the seat of the country's ancient kings, and also a derivation of the Aramaic 'to throw' or 'carry'.
VARIANTS: Tarrah, Taryn, Tatiana

Tatum

Possibly a feminine version of Tate, from the Middle English for 'cheerful' and 'spirited', or from the Old English for a variety of other words, including 'dear', 'dice', 'hilltop', 'tress of hair' and 'treat'. Also believed to come from the Native American for 'windy' or 'garrulous'.
VARIANTS: Tait, Tata, Tayte

Taylor

Originally an occupational surname for a cutter of cloth, from the Anglo-Norman 'tailler', meaning 'to cut'.

Temp

A short form of Tempest, an Old French name meaning 'storm', and of Temperance, a Christian virtue that means 'moderation'.
VARIANTS: Temperance, Tempest, Tempesta, Tempeste, Tempestt

Terri

Feminine variant of Terence, derived from the Old Roman name Terentius, and also a short form of Theresa, a Greek name associated with 'harvest time'.
VARIANTS: Teresa, Teri, Theresa

Thalia

From the Greek word 'thallein' which means 'to flourish'.
VARIANTS: Talia, Talya, Thali

Theresa

A name of Greek origin, associated with late summer and the harvest.
VARIANTS: Teresa, Terri, Tess, Tessa, Thérèse, Theresia, Tracy, Tracey

Tia

As a pet form of Christina this means 'Christian', but as a variant of Titiana it means 'fairy queen'.
VARIANTS: Christina, Christine, Tania, Tanya, Tatiana, Tina

Tina

Originally a pet form of Christina, which means 'Christian', and also used as a short form for other names ending in 'tina', such as Valentina.
VARIANTS: Christina, Christine, Tatiana, Tia, Tiana, Tyna

Toni

A short form of Antonia, from the Old Roman family name Antonius, which may have come from the Greek for 'flourishing' or 'flower'.
VARIANTS: Antonia, Tonie, Tonya

Tracy

A pet form of Theresa, or a variant of the Gaelic Treacy, meaning 'warlike'.
VARIANTS: Teresa, Terese, Theresa, Thérèse, Trace, Tracey, Tracie

Tyler

From the Old English occupational surname for someone who was a tiler.

Uma

The name of the Hindu goddess of beauty and sunlight.

Ursula

From the Latin for 'little bear'. It is also the feminine equivalent of the name Orson ('bear').
VARIANTS: Orsa, Orsola, Ursala, Urse, Ursel, Ursie, Ursola

Valentina

The feminine form of Valentine, from the Latin for 'healthy', 'strong' and 'vigorous'.
VARIANTS: Valeria, Valerie

Valerie

Also derived from the Latin 'valens' meaning 'healthy', 'strong' and 'vigorous'.
VARIANTS: Val, Valaree, Valari, Valeria, Valery, Valentina

Vanessa

Thought to be the invention of the 18th century writer Jonathan Swift, who used it as a nickname for his friend Esther Vanhomrigh.
VARIANTS: Nessa, Nessie, Van, Vania, Vannie, Vanny

Venus

The Roman goddess of love and the second planet from the sun.
VARIANTS: Venita, Vin, Vinita, Vinnie

Verity

A Christian virtue, from the Old French and Latin words for 'truth'.
VARIANTS: Vera, Verena

Veronica

A saint's name, from the Latin for 'true image'. Veronica is the patron saint of photographers.
VARIANTS: Berenice, Bernice, Nika, Ron, Roni, Verenice, Verona, Veronika, Veronique, Vonni

Victoria

An eternally popular name from the Latin for 'victory'.
VARIANTS: Tora, Tori, Tory, Vic, Vicci, Vicki, Vicky, Victoire, Victoriana, Victorina

Violet

A colour and a flower of deep reddish blue.
VARIANTS: Viola, Violetta

Virginia

An American state, named after Elizabeth I of England, 'the Virgin Queen'.
VARIANTS: Gina, Ginger, Ginia, Ginni, Ginny, Virgie, Virginie

Vivian

From the Old French word for 'full of life'.
VARIANTS: Vivi, Vivien, Vivienne, Vyvian, Vyvyan

Wendy

The invention of JM Barrie, the author of 'Peter Pan', inspired by a child called Margaret Henley who called him 'my friendy -wendy'.
VARIANTS: Wanda, Wenda, Wendi, Wendie

Whitney

Originally a Middle English place name meaning 'by the white island'.
VARIANTS: Whitnee, Whitni, Whitnie, Whitny, Witney

Willow

The willow is pliant and graceful and it is from this tree that the girls' name is derived.

Winona

From the Old High German and Old English for 'blissfully happy', and also a Native American name and place name meaning 'firstborn daughter'.
VARIANTS: Wenona, Wenonah, Winnie, Wynona

Yasmin

The Arabic variant of Jasmine, derived from the sweet-smelling jasmine flower.
VARIANTS: Jasmine, Yasmina, Yasmine

Yoko

From the Japanese for 'positive' and 'female'.

Yolanda

Derived from the Greek word 'ion', which means 'violet', the Latin meaning of Yolanda is 'modest'.
VARIANTS: Iolanthe, Violet, Yolande

Yvette

The feminine version of Yves and a diminutive of Yvonne, of French and Old German derivation, meaning 'yew'.
VARIANTS: Ivetta, Yevette, Yve, Yvonne

Yvonne

From the French and Old German word for 'yew', it is associated with archery.
VARIANTS: Evona, Evonne, Ivetta, Yevette, Yve, Yvette

Zara

A name of Arabic origin meaning 'flower' or 'brightness' and 'splendour of the dawn'. Also a variant of Sarah, from the Hebrew for 'princess'.
VARIANTS: Sara, Sarah, Zahra, Zarah

Zita

From the Italian for 'child'.
VARIANTS: Citha, Rosita, Sitha, Zeta

Zoe

A variant of Eve, from the Greek translation of the Hebrew word for 'life'.
VARIANTS: Eva, Eve, Evie, Evita, Vita, Zoë, Zoey, Zowie

Zola

From the Latin meaning 'earth', and also an African name meaning 'tranquil'.
VARIANT: Zoe

Boys'
Names

Aaron

From the Hebrew for 'mountain of strength' or 'brightness', Aaron also means 'messenger' in Arabic.
VARIANTS: Aharon, Ahron, Ari, Arnie, Aron, Arron, Haroun, Ron, Ronnie

Abdul

A short form of Abdullah, which means 'servant of Allah' in Arabic.
VARIANTS: Ab, Abdal, Abdel, Abdullah

Abel

Abel has two possible Hebrew meanings: 'son' or 'source of God', or 'herdsman'.
VARIANTS: Abelard, Abeles, Abell, Able

Abir

In Hebrew this name means 'strong' and 'heroic'.
VARIANTS: Abira, Amoz, Amzi, Azaz, Aziz, Aziza

Abner

This name means 'father of light' or 'my father is light' in Hebrew.
VARIANTS: Ab, Abbey, Abby

Abraham

The name Abraham means 'father of many' or 'father of a multitude'.
VARIANTS: Ab, Abe, Abi, Abie, Abrahan, Bram, Ham, Ibrahim

Absalom

Absalom is a name from the Old Testament and means 'father of peace'.
VARIANTS: Absolun, Axel

Adam

The Hebrew meaning of Adam is 'earth'.
VARIANTS: Ad, Adamo, Adamson, Addie, Adom, Edom

Adrian

The name Adrian, like the Adriatic Sea, is derived from the Latin word 'ater' meaning 'black'.
VARIANTS: Ade, Adriano, Adrien, Hadrian

Adriel

In Hebrew this name means 'God's majesty' or 'one of God's congregation'.
VARIANTS: Adri, Adrial

Ahmed

An Arabic name meaning 'greatly adored' or 'praised the most'.
VARIANT: Ahmad

Aidan

From the Irish Gaelic for 'little fiery one', and also from Latin roots, meaning 'to help'.
VARIANTS: Aden, Aiden, Aodán, Aodham, Edan, Eden

Ainsley

Derived from the Old English meaning 'my meadow or land'.
VARIANTS: Ainie, Ainslee, Ainslie

Alan

An Old Celtic name that means 'harmony'. It may also come from the Irish Gaelic for 'good-looking' and 'cheerful', and has the Breton meaning 'rock'.
VARIANTS: Al, Allan, Allen, Alleyn, Alyn

Aled

Aled is the name of a river in Wales. It means 'offspring' or 'noble brow'.
VARIANT: Al

Alexander

A heroic name that comes from the Greek Alexandros, which means 'defender of men'.

VARIANTS: Al, Alec, Aleksander, Alex, Alexei, Alexis, Ali, Alistair, Sacha, Sandy

Alfred

This name of a famous king of England comes from the Old English for 'good counsel' or 'elf counsel'.

VARIANTS: Alf, Alfie, Fred, Freddie

Alistair

An alternative spelling of the Gaelic Alasdair, which is a version of the Greek name Alexandros – more commonly known as Alexander – and means 'defender of men' or 'warrior'.

VARIANTS: Alasdair, Alastair, Alexander, Alister

Alphonse

From the Old High German for 'noble' and 'ready' or 'apt'.

VARIANTS: Al, Alfonso, Alphonsine, Alphonso, Fons, Fonsie, Fonz

Ambrose

From the Greek meaning 'divine' or 'immortal'.

VARIANTS: Ambie, Ambros, Ambrosio, Ambrosius, Brose

Amir

This is an Arabic name which means 'prince'.

Variant: Emir

Amos

A biblical name which means 'to carry', 'bearer of a burden' or 'troubled'.

Andrew

A name of Greek origin, which means 'manly'.

VARIANTS: Anders, Anderson, André, Andreas, Andrei, Andres, Andy

Angus

A form of the Gaelic name Aonghus, which means 'one choice'.

VARIANTS: Aengus, Ennis, Gus

Anthony

From the Old Roman family name Antonius, thought to have been derived from the Greek for 'flourishing'.

VARIANTS: Antoine, Anton, Antonio, Antony, Toni, Tonio, Tony

Anton

The French form of Anthony, which may come from the Greek for 'flourishing' or the Roman for 'priceless'.

VARIANTS: Anthony, Antoine, Antonio, Antony, Toni, Tonio, Tony

Archie

Short for Archibald, which comes from the Germanic for 'noble' and 'bold'.

VARIANTS: Archibald, Archy

Ardal

An Irish name that stems from the words for 'high valour'. It may also mean 'bear'.

VARIANTS: Ardgal, Ardghal

Arden

From the Latin for 'to be on fire', 'ablaze', 'sparkle', 'glitter' and 'dazzle'.

VARIANTS: Ard, Arda, Ardie, Ardin, Ardy

Arnold

A Germanic name that means 'eagle' and 'rule'.

VARIANTS: Armand, Armant, Arn, Arnald, Arnaud, Arnie, Arny

Arthur

This legendary name is thought to stem from the Greek for 'bear-keeper' or the Celtic for 'bear'. Equally it could mean 'stone' or 'rock' in Irish Gaelic, 'noble' in Welsh or 'follower of Thor' in Norse. A link between Arthur and the Roman family name Artorius has also been suggested.
VARIANTS: Art, Arth, Artie, Arty

Asher

This biblical name means 'happy' in Hebrew. It is also thought to mean 'martial', while the Swahili interpretation is 'born during Asher' (a Muslim month).

Ashley

From the Old English for 'ash' and 'wood', Ashley would have been given to someone who lived in or near an ash wood.
VARIANTS: Ashlie, Ashly

Ashton

Like Ashley, Ashton is derived from the Old English for 'ash tree', and 'tun', meaning 'enclosure' or 'settlement'.

Auberon

An Old French name meaning 'noble' and 'like a bear'. It is also a pet form of Aubrey.
VARIANTS: Alberic, Aubery, Oberon

Aubrey

A Norman French name taken from the Germanic Alberic, which means 'elf-ruler'.
VARIANTS: Alberic, Alberich, Aubary, Auberon, Aubri, Aubry

Avi

This name comes from the Hebrew for 'my father' and is traditionally used in reference to 'God'.
VARIANTS: Abi, Av, Avodal

Axel

In German Axel means 'oak' or 'small oak tree', but it may also come from the Scandinavian for 'divine reward', or can be a variant of the biblical name Absalom.
VARIANTS: Absalom, Aksel

Azaria

A Hebrew name which means 'God is my help'.
VARIANTS: Azariah, Azriel

Bailey

See *Bailey* in the Girls' section.

Barclay

From Berkeley, a place in Gloucestershire, which in Old English means 'birch-tree' and 'wood' or 'clearing'.

Barnabas

A biblical name of Aramaic origin, which means 'son of consolation' or 'son of exhortation'.
VARIANTS: Barn, Barnabe, Barnaby, Barnie

Barry

This name has four possible origins. One is from the Gaelic name Bearrach, which means 'spear' or 'good marksman'. Another is from the Welsh for 'son of Harry'. It is also a short form of the Irish name Finbar, which means 'fair head'. And finally it relates to a Welsh place name – Barry Island – 'bar' meaning 'dune' or 'mound'.
VARIANTS: Bari, Barnard, Barnett, Barra, Barrie, Barrington, Barrymore, Baz, Bazza, Finbar

Bartholomew

In Hebrew Bartholomew simply means 'son of Talmai', who was one of Christ's Apostles.
VARIANTS: Bart, Bartel, Bartholomieu, Bartlett, Bartley, Barty, Bate, Tolly, Tolomieu, Tolomey

Baxter

Originally used as a surname, Baxter comes from the Old English for 'baker'.

Beasley

From the Old English for 'field of peas'.
VARIANT: Peasley

Beau

A French name which means 'handsome'.
VARIANT: Beauregard

Benedict

The Latin meaning of Benedict is 'blessed'.
VARIANTS: Ben, Benedicto, Benes, Beniton, Bennett, Benny, Dick, Dixie

Bentley

From the Old English meaning 'clearing of bent grass'. Another possible meaning is 'to exist' or 'to become'.
VARIANTS: Ben, Benny, Bently

Bernard

An Old French name which means 'to be as bold or brave as a bear'.
VARIANTS: Barnard, Barnet, Barney, Bernardo, Bernhard, Bernhardt, Bernie, Björn

Blain

From the Gaelic word for 'yellow', used to refer to someone with blond hair. It can also mean 'narrow' or 'servant of St Blane'.
VARIANTS: Blaine, Blane, Blayne

Blair

Originally a place name, Blair comes from the Gaelic for 'plain', 'field' or 'battle'.
VARIANTS: Blaire, Blayre

Blake

From two Old English words with opposite meanings: 'blæc' meaning 'black' and 'blac' meaning 'pale' or 'white', used in reference to hair or complexion.
VARIANTS: Blanchard, Blanco

Benjamin

This popular Jewish name means 'son of my right hand' and 'son of the south' in Hebrew.
VARIANTS: Ben, Benjy, Bennie, Benny

Bodi

A Hungarian name which means 'may God protect the king'.

Boris

From the Slavonic for 'battle' or 'stranger', Boris also has the Tartar meaning of 'small'.
VARIANT: Borislav

Boyd

The name of a clan in Scotland, which comes from the Gaelic for 'yellow hair'.
VARIANTS: Bow, Bowen, Bowie

Brad

A pet form of the Irish Bradley, meaning 'descendant of Brádach', and also the Old English Braden, meaning 'to broaden', 'make spacious' or 'plain-spoken'.
VARIANTS: Bradd, Braden, Bradford, Bradleigh, Bradley, Brady

Brady

Like Bradley, the name Brady comes from the Gaelic for 'descendant of Brádach'.
VARIANTS: Brad, Bradd, Bradleigh, Bradley

Brandon

From the Old English for 'broom' and 'hill', or from the Middle English for 'torch', 'fire' or 'sword'.
VARIANTS: Branden, Brandt, Brant, Brendan, Brent

Brent

Brent's Celtic meaning is 'high place' or 'hill', while the Old English interpretation is 'burned'.
VARIANTS: Brendt, Brenten, Brenton

Brett

From the Old French for 'a Breton or Briton'.
VARIANTS: Bret, Bretton, Brit, Briton, Britton

Brian

From the Celtic king Brian Boru, whose name meant 'strong', 'hill' or 'elevated'.
VARIANTS: Briant, Briar, Bryan, Bryant

Brice

From the Welsh 'son of Rhys' or from the German for 'rich' and 'wealthy'.
VARIANTS: Bryce, Bryson, Bryston

Brock

The Old English meaning of the name Brock is 'badger'.
VARIANTS: Badger, Braxton, Brook

Bruce

Its exact meaning is uncertain, but Bruce may come from the French for 'wood' or 'copse'.
VARIANTS: Brucey, Brucie, Bruis, Brus

Bruno

The German meaning of the name Bruno is 'bear' or 'brown like a bear'.
VARIANTS: Bronson, Bruin, Bruna, Bruns

Bryn

From the Welsh for 'hill', Bryn is also a short form of the name Brynmor – a place.
VARIANTS: Brinn, Brynn

Bryson

A variant of the name Brice, which means 'son of Rhys' in Welsh or 'rich, wealthy' and 'powerful ruler' in German. It is also an Anglicised version of the Irish surname Ó Briosáin.
VARIANTS: Brice, Bryce

Buck

From the Old English meaning 'stag', 'male deer' and 'he-goat'.

Bud

From 'buddy', the English for 'friend' or 'brother'.
VARIANTS: Budd, Buddy

Burgess

From the Latin for 'fortified place'. In Old French it was used to describe a free man in a borough or town.
VARIANT: Burgiss

Burr

The Middle English meaning of this name is 'rough edge', but the Scandinavian interpretation is 'youth'.
VARIANTS: Burbank, Burrell, Burris, Burton

Burt

A variant of Bert, which is the short form of a variety of names and comes from the Old English for 'bright'.
VARIANTS: Albert, Bert, Bertram, Cuthbert, Egbert, Gilbert, Herbert, Lambert, Osbert, Robert

Burton

From the Old English words 'burh' and 'tun' and means 'fortress' and 'enclosure' or 'fortified place' and 'settlement'.

Byron

From the Old English for 'cow shed' or 'cattle herder'.
VARIANTS: Biron, Byram, Byrom

Cahil
This Turkish name means 'young' and 'naïve'.

Caleb
An Old Testament name whose Hebrew meaning is 'bold' or 'without fear'.
VARIANTS: Cal, Cale, Kalb, Kale, Kaleb, Kalev

Callum
From the saint's name Columba, which means 'dove'.
VARIANTS: Calum, Colm, Colum, Kallum, Kalum, Malcolm

Calvin
The meaning of Calvin is derived from the French for 'bald' or 'little bald one'.
VARIANTS: Cal, Vin, Vinny

Cameron
A Scottish surname whose meaning comes from the Gaelic for 'crooked nose'.
VARIANTS: Cam, Camaron, Camron, Kam, Kamaron, Kameron, Kamron

Carl
This Old German name is a form of Charles, which means 'man'.
VARIANTS: Carlo, Carlos, Charles, Karl

Carlton
An Old English surname and place name that is derived from two words: 'carl', meaning 'free man or peasant', and 'tun', 'town' or 'settlement'.
VARIANTS: Carl, Carleton, Carlson, Charles, Charlton

Carson
Possibly of English derivation, meaning 'son of Carr', or a reference to someone who lived in a marsh.

Carter
From the Old Norse for 'cart for transporting goods' and 'driver of a cart'.

Cary
Pronounced 'Carry', this has various possible origins, including the Irish for 'son of the dark one', the Welsh meaning 'castle dweller' and the Latin meaning 'much loved' and 'costly'.
VARIANTS: Carey, Charles

Caspian
The exact meaning of the name is unclear, but it is the name of the stretch of water known as the Caspian Sea.

Cassius
From the Greek for 'herb' and the Italian for 'cinnamon bark'. In Latin it means 'vain'.
VARIANTS: Case, Casey, Cash, Casius, Cass, Cassie, Cassy, Kas

Chad
The modern variant of the Old English saint's name Ceadda, which meant 'martial'.
VARIANTS: Chadd, Chaddie, Chaddy, Chadwick

Chandler
An occupational name from the French for 'candle maker' or 'seller of candles'.
VARIANTS: Chan, Chaney, Cheney, Shandler

Charles
From the Old German for 'man' or 'free man'.
VARIANTS: Carl, Carlos, Carlton, Charley, Charlie, Charlton, Chas, Chaz, Chuck, Karl

Chip
The short form of Christopher, which comes from the Greek 'one who carries Christ'. It also comes from the name of a Native American tribe, the Chippewa.
VARIANTS: Chipper, Christopher

Christian

The literal meaning is 'follower of Christ', but in Greek it means 'anointed one', a direct translation of the Hebrew term 'Messiah'.
VARIANTS: Chris, Christiaan, Christiano, Christie, Christien, Kit, Kris, Kristian

Christobal

A combination of two words, 'Christ' and 'ball', thus 'dance of Christ'.
VARIANTS: Cristobal

Christopher

The saint's name Christopher comes from the Greek for 'one who carries Christ'.
VARIANTS: Chip, Chris, Chrissie, Christoph, Christophe, Kester, Kit, Kristofer

Clark

Originally an occupational name for someone who earned a living by his ability to read or write.
VARIANTS: Clarke, Claxton

Claude

From the Roman family name Claudius, which in Latin means 'limping' or 'lame'.
VARIANTS: Claudell, Claudian, Claudius, Claus

Claus

As a variant of Claudius, Claus means 'limp', 'lame', 'crippled' or 'defective', but it is also a German form of the name Nicholas, which comes from the Greek for 'people's victory'.
VARIANTS: Claude, Claudell, Claudian, Claudius, Klaus, Nicholas

Clay

From the Old English word for 'clay' or 'fine-grained earth'. It is also a short form of Clayton, which means 'town on clay land'.
VARIANTS: Clayland, Clayton, Cle, Clea, Cletus, Klay

Clement

This name comes from the Latin for 'kind', 'gentle', 'calm' and 'merciful'.
VARIANTS: Clem, Cleme, Clemen, Clemens, Clemmy

Clinton

A family name, which comes from the Middle English for 'hilltop town'.
VARIANT: Clint

Clive

From the Old English for 'overhanging rock face', 'cliff' or 'slope'.
VARIANTS: Cleve, Cleveland, Clevey, Clevie, Cliff, Clifton

Clyde

The name of a Scottish river, derived from the Celtic meaning 'to wash'. It also comes from the Welsh for 'heard from far away'.
VARIANTS: Cly, Clydesdale, Clywd

Cody

Originally an Irish surname that means 'descendant of a helpful or cheerful person'.
VARIANTS: Codi, Codie

Cole

Derived from the Middle English for 'coal', this also comes from the Welsh for 'trust'. Furthermore it can be used as a pet form of Nicholas, which means 'people's victory' in Greek.
VARIANTS: Colby, Coleman, Colin, Collie, Collier, Collis, Colton, Colville, Colvin, Nicholas

Colin

A short form of Nicholas, meaning 'people's victory', or from the Scottish Gaelic for 'youth' and 'puppy' and the Irish Gaelic for 'young man'. 'Chieftain' is another Celtic meaning.
VARIANTS: Cailean, Colan, Cole, Collie, Collin, Collins, Colly, Colyn, Nicholas

Connor

A shortened form of the Irish legendary figure Conchobhar, whose name means 'lover of hounds'.
VARIANTS: Conn, Conor

Conrad

A German name meaning 'wise counsel'.
VARIANTS: Con, Curt, Konrad, Kurt

Corbin

Thought to be derived from the Old French for 'raven' or from the Anglo-Norman for 'crow'.
VARIANTS: Corban, Corben, Corbet, Corbett, Corby, Corbyn, Korbin, Korby

Corey

The Greek meaning of Corey is 'helmet', but it also comes from the Irish and Scottish Gaelic for 'hollow dweller' or 'pool dweller'.
VARIANTS: Cori, Correy, Corry, Cory, Korey, Kori, Kory

Cormac

Cormac comes from the Greek for 'tree trunk', but may also mean 'charioteer' and 'son of the raven' in Irish Gaelic.
VARIANTS: Cormack, Cormick

Cosmo

From the Greek for 'order' or 'beauty'.
VARIANTS: Cosimo, Cosmas

Craig

The Anglicised form of the Scottish Gaelic family name meaning 'from the rocks'.
VARIANT: Kraig

Cramer

From the Old English for 'to squeeze' or 'to fill up'. It was usually associated with cramming one's head with knowledge or filling the stomach with food.
VARIANTS: Cram, Kramer

Crispin

Derived from the Latin for 'curly' and would have originally been a reference to a person's hair.
VARIANTS: Crispinian, Crispus, Krispin

Crosby

From the Old Norse for 'from the place with the cross' and from the Middle English for 'cross'.
VARIANTS: Crosbey, Crosbie

Curtis

Originally a surname derived from the Latin for 'courtyard', Curtis is also related to the Old French meaning 'to be courtly or courteous', and the Old English for 'short stockings'.
VARIANTS: Court, Courtenay, Courtland, Courts, Curt, Kurt, Kurtis

Cyrus

Cyrus was the founder of the Persian Empire and his name means 'sun' or 'throne'.
VARIANTS: Ciro, Cy, Cyrie, Cyro, Kir, Russ, Sy

Dahi

Although thought of as a variant of David, it is a Welsh name that comes from the Celtic for 'nimble'.

Dalai

From the Sanskrit for 'mediator'.

Dale

From the Old Norse for 'broad valley' and the Old English for 'valley'.
VARIANTS: Dal, Daley, Dali, Dalton, Dayle, Delles, Dillon

Damon

Several meanings are attributed to the name Damon, including the Greek for 'fate' or 'divine power' and the Old English for 'day'. It is also linked to the Latin for 'evil spirit' or 'demon'.
VARIANTS: Dame, Damian, Damiano, Damien, Dayman

Daniel

This popular Hebrew name means 'God is my judge'.
VARIANTS: Dan, Dana, Dane, Daneil, Dani, Dannie, Danny, Dano, Deiniol

Dante

From the Italian for 'to endure, bear or be patient'. It is also the short form of the name Durante, from the Latin for 'steadfast'.
VARIANTS: Devonte, Donte, Duran, Durant, Durante

Darcy

See *Darcie* in the Girls' section.

Darius

A Persian name meaning 'protector', but also Greek for 'wealthy' or 'rich'.
VARIANTS: Daare, Daren, Daria, Darian, Darien, Dario, Darren

Darren

As a variant of Darius, Darren is derived from the Greek for 'rich' or the Persian for 'protector'. It may also come from an Irish name meaning 'great' or 'small one'.
VARIANTS: Dar, Daren, Darien, Darin, Dario, Darius, Darnell, Daryn

Darwin

From Old English meaning 'lover of the sea'.
VARIANTS: Dar, Derwin, Derwyn, Durwin

David

A Biblical name which means 'beloved' in Hebrew.
VARIANTS: Dafydd, Dahi, Dai, Dave, Daveed, Davi, Davide, Davy

De Angelo

From the Greek for 'angel' or 'messenger'.
VARIANTS: Angel, Angelo, DeAngelo

Dean

From the Old English for 'valley', the Middle English 'dene' for an ecclesiastical supervisor, or from the Greek for 'ten'.
VARIANTS: Dene, Denn, Dino

Declan

Possibly derived from the Irish Gaelic for 'good'.
VARIANT: Deaglan

Delmar

From the Latin meaning 'of the sea'.
VARIANTS: Del, Delmer, Delmore

Delvin

Derived from the Greek word 'delphis', which means 'dolphin'.
VARIANTS: Del, Delwin

Dennis

A French name derived from Dionysus, the Greek god of wine.
VARIANTS: Deenys, Den, Denis, Denison, Dennison, Denny, Denys, Dion, Dionysius

Denver

Originally an Old English place name meaning 'Danes' crossing'. In Middle English it means 'little forested valley'.
VARIANTS: Den, Dennie, Denny

Denzel

Taken from the Cornish place name Denzell, from the Celtic for 'stronghold' and the Old Cornish for 'high'.
VARIANTS: Denzell, Denzil

Dermot

An Irish name which means 'without injunction' or 'free from envy'.
VARIANTS: Darby, Derby, Dermod, Dermott, Diarmid, Diarmod, Diarmuid

Desmond

From the Latin meaning 'of or from the world', or the Irish Gaelic meaning 'from south Munster' or 'descendant of one from south Munster'.
VARIANTS: Des, Desi, Dezi

Devon

An English county, which took its name from the Celtic Dumnonii tribe who lived there.
VARIANTS: Devan, Deven, Devin, Devyn

Dexter

Originally a surname from the Latin for 'right-sided' or 'right-handed'.
VARIANTS: Decca, Deck, Dek, Dex

Dhani

A Hindu name which means 'person of wealth and riches'.

Didi

Short for the French Didier, which derives its meaning from the Latin for 'ardent desire', 'deep longing' and 'wish'.
VARIANTS: Didier, Didon, Didot, Dizier, Dodo

Diego

The Spanish form of the biblical name James, which is itself a variant of the Old Testament name Jacob, which means 'supplanter'.
VARIANTS: Jacob, James

Digby

An English place name from the French for 'to dig a ditch or dike' and the Old Norse for 'ditch' and 'settlement'.

Dirk

In Scotland 'dirk' is another word for 'dagger'. The name is also the Dutch and Flemish form of Derek, which comes from the Old High German for 'famous ruler' or 'the people's ruler'.
VARIANTS: Derek, Derrick

Dominic

From the Latin meaning 'of the Lord', traditionally bestowed upon boys born on a Sunday.
VARIANTS: Dom, Domenic, Domenico, Domenyk, Domingo, Dominick, Nick, Nickie, Nicky

Donald

The Anglicised version of the Celtic Domhnall, which means 'global or proud ruler'.
VARIANTS: Domhnall, Don, Donahue, Donal, Donaldo, Donalt, Donn, Donne, Donnie, Donovan

Donnel

From the Gaelic for 'hill' or 'hill fort', but also a variant of Donald, meaning 'global or proud ruler'.
VARIANTS: Don, Donald, Donn, Donnell, Donnelly, Donny, Dun

Donovan

An Irish surname which means 'descendant of Donndubhán', a personal name for someone of dark complexion.
VARIANTS: Don, Donavan, Donnie, Donny, Van

Dorian

In Ancient Greece a Dorian was someone who came from the Doris region. Doris meant 'bountiful sea' or 'sacrificial knife'. Alternatively Dorian may come from the Greek word for 'gift', 'doron'.
VARIANTS: Doran, Dore, Dorey, Dorie, Doron, Dory

Dougal

From the Irish Gaelic meaning 'dark stranger'.
VARIANTS: Doug, Dougie, Doyle, Dug, Dugard, Duggy, Dughall

Douglas

Derived from the Gaelic, meaning 'black stream'.
VARIANTS: Doug, Dougal, Dougie, Douglass, Dougy, Dugald, Duggie

Doyle

As a variant of Dougal, Doyle means 'dark stranger', but it also comes from the Irish Gaelic for 'assembly' or 'gathering'.
VARIANT: Dougal

Drake

From the Greek for 'serpent' or 'dragon'.

Dudley

From the Old English for 'Duddha's clearing or wood'.
VARIANTS: Dud, Dudd, Dudly

Duke

From the Latin for 'leader, conductor', 'guide' or 'commander'. Also a hereditary title of nobility, like 'earl'.

Duncan

From the Scottish Gaelic words 'donn' ('greyish-brown') and 'chadh' ('warrior') to mean 'dark-skinned warrior'.
VARIANTS: Dun, Dunc, Dune, Dunkie, Dunn

Dustin

Either from the German for 'warrior' or the Old Norse for 'Thor's stone'.
VARIANTS: Dust, Dustie, Dusty

Dwayne

Derives from the Irish Gaelic for 'dark little one'.
VARIANTS: Duane, Duwayne, Dwain

Dwight

From the Old English for 'white, fair'.
VARIANTS: DeWitt, Dewitt, Diot, Doyt, Wit, Wittie, Witty

Dylan

Possibly derived from the Celtic word for 'sea'.
VARIANTS: Dillan, Dillon

Eamon

The Irish Gaelic form of Edmund, from the Old English for 'happiness', 'riches' and 'protector'. Also a variant of Edward.
VARIANTS: Eamonn, Edmund, Edward

Earl

This name means 'nobleman', 'chief', 'prince' or 'warrior' in Old English.
VARIANTS: Earle, Erle

Eden

May be a variant of Aidan, which means 'little fiery one' in Irish Gaelic, or it could come from the Old English for 'prosperity, riches' and 'bear cub'.
VARIANTS: Aidan, Ed, Edan, Eddie, Eddy

Edgar

This name comes from the Old English for 'lucky spear'.
VARIANTS: Ed, Eddie

Edmund

The Old English meaning of the name Edmund is 'happy protection'.
VARIANTS: Eadmond, Eamon, Ed, Eddie, Eddy, Edmond, Esmund, Ned, Ted, Teddy

Edward

A name that comes from the Old English for 'happy', 'fortunate', 'rich' and 'guardian' or 'protector'.
VARIANTS: Eamon, Ed, Eddie, Eddy, Edison, Eduardo, Ned, Neddie, Ted, Teddy

Edwin

A combination of two Old English words, 'eadig' meaning 'fortunate, prosperous, happy', and 'wine' meaning 'friend'.
VARIANTS: Eaduin, Ed, Edred, Edwyn, Neddie, Teddy

Elan

There are three meanings for the name Elan: from the Latin for 'spirited', the Hebrew for 'tree' or the Native American for 'friendly'.
VARIANTS: Ela, Elai

Eli

Although Eli is often used as a pet form of the names Elijah ('the Lord is my God') and Elisha ('God is my help'), it is actually a name in its own right, meaning 'elevated', 'height' or 'Jehovah'.
VARIANTS: El, Eloy, Ely, Ilie

Elliott

As a variant of Elias, the Greek form of Elijah, Elliott comes from the Hebrew for 'the Lord is my God'. It is also a surname derived from the Old English for 'noble battle'.
VARIANTS: Eli, Elias, Elijah, Eliot, Ellis

Ellis

Believed to have come from the biblical name Elijah, which means 'the Lord is my God', Ellis may equally derive from the Welsh for 'benevolent'.
VARIANTS: Eli, Elias, Elie, Elis, Ellison, Elly, Elson, Elston, Ely

Elmer

From the Old English name Aethelmaer, which means 'noble' and 'famous'.
VARIANTS: Ailemar, Aylmer, Edmar, Edmer, Eilemar, Elma, Elmo, Elmore

Elmo

A variant of Elmer, and also the pet form of Erasmus, from the Greek for 'beloved' or 'desired'.
VARIANTS: Elmer, Erasme, Erasmus

Elroy
From the Spanish and French for 'the king'.

Elton
An English family name that comes from the Old English for 'Ella's settlement' or 'noble town'.
VARIANTS: Elden, Elsdom, Elston

Elvis
Possibly a variant of Elvin, which comes from the Old English for 'elf-like'.
VARIANTS: Alby, Alvin, Elli, Elly, Elvin

Emmanuel
This biblical name comes from the Hebrew for 'God is with us'.
VARIANTS: Emanuel, Emanuele, Immanuel, Mani, Manny, Manuel, Manuela

Emmett
Taken from the Hebrew for 'truth' and the Old English for 'ant'.
VARIANTS: Emmet, Emmit, Emmitt

Emyr
A Welsh name which means 'ruler, king or lord'.

Eric
A Scandinavian name of Old Norse in origin, meaning 'honourable ruler', 'one ruler' or 'island ruler'.
VARIANTS: Erik, Eryk, Euric, Ric, Rick, Rickie, Ricky

Errol
Possibly a variant of the Welsh name Eryl, which means 'watcher' or 'a lookout post', or of Harold, which comes from the Old German for 'army leader'. It may also be a Scottish family name that was taken from a Scottish place name, or a German form of Earl.
VARIANTS: Earl, Erroll, Harold, Rollo, Rolly

Esau
A biblical name from the Hebrew for 'hairy'.

Esmond
From the Old English for 'grace, beauty' and 'protector'.

Ethan
The biblical name Ethan comes from the Hebrew for 'permanent' and 'assured'.
VARIANTS: Etan, Ethe

Euan
A Welsh form of John, which means 'God is gracious', but also a Celtic version of Eugene, from the Greek for 'well-born'.
VARIANTS: Eugene, Ewan, Ewen, Owain, Owen

Eugene
From the Greek for 'noble' or 'well-born'.
VARIANTS: Eugen, Eugenio, Eugenius, Ewan, Ewen, Gene, Owain, Owen

Ezekiel
A biblical name from the Hebrew for 'may God strengthen'.
VARIANTS: Ezechial, Ezell, Haskell, Hehezhel, Zeke

Ezra
This Old Testament name means 'help' in Hebrew.
VARIANTS: Azariah, Azur, Esdras, Ezar, Ezer, Ezera, Ezri

Fabian
Derived from the Latin for 'bean'.
VARIANTS: Fabe, Faber, Fabiano, Fabien, Fabio, Fabius

Fadil
From the Arabic for 'virtuous' and 'distinguished'.

Fahey
From the Old English for 'joyful, glad' and 'happy'.

Farley
Possibly from the Old French for 'fair', as in 'celebration', or from the Old Norse for 'beautiful or pleasing'. Alternatively it may be derived from the Old English for 'wayside' or the Middle English for 'meadow'.
VARIANTS: Fair, Fairbanks, Fairleigh, Fairley, Far, Farl, Farlie, Farly

Farrell
A variant of the Irish name Fergal, which means 'valiant man', and the Latin Farrar, which means 'blacksmith' or 'iron'.
VARIANTS: Farrel, Farris, Fergal, Ferris, Ferrol

Felix

From the Latin for 'happy' or 'lucky'.
VARIANTS: Felice, Felike

Fergal

Anglicised form of the Gaelic name meaning 'man of valour'.
VARIANTS: Farrell, Ferghal

Fergus

This popular saints' name is usually taken to mean 'best or manly choice' in Gaelic. It can also mean 'vigorous man'.
VARIANTS: Feargus, Fergie, Ferguson, Fergy

Fidel

A Spanish name derived from the Latin for 'faithful' and 'trust'.
VARIANTS: Fidele, Fidelio

Finbar

Anglicised form of the Irish Fionnbharr, which means 'fair-headed'.
VARIANTS: Barry, Fin, Findlay, Finley, Finn

Finlay

This Scottish surname comes from the Gaelic for 'fair-haired soldier'.
VARIANTS: Fin, Findlay, Findley, Finley, Finn

Fitzgerald

From the Norman French meaning 'son' and Gerald comes from the Old German for 'spear rule'.
VARIANT: Fitz

Fletcher

Originally an occupational name for someone who made arrows.
VARIANT: Fletch

Flint

The word 'flint' means 'hard rock' in Middle English.

Floyd

A variant of the Welsh name Lloyd, which means 'grey'.
VARIANT: Lloyd

Flynn

The Gaelic meaning of this name is 'son of the red-haired man'.
VARIANTS: Flin, Flinn

Forbes

The Irish Gaelic interpretation of this name is 'field owner' or 'prosperous'.

Forrest

Transferred surname originally given to someone who lived near a wood.
VARIANTS: Forest, Forester, Foster

Francis

The original meaning of this name was 'the little Frenchman' or 'with the airs and graces of a Frenchman'.
VARIANTS: Franc, Francesco, Francisco, Franck, Franco, François, Frank, Frankie

Fraser

This may be derived from the French word for 'strawberry', or for 'charcoal cinders' or 'charcoal maker'.
VARIANTS: Frasier, Frazer, Frazier

Frederick

From the Old High German for 'peaceful ruler'.
VARIANTS: Eric, Erick, Fred, Freddie, Freddy, Frederic, Frederik, Fridrich, Rick, Rickie

Fuller

Originally an occupational name for someone who shrinks and thickens cloth.

Gabriel

This angelic name means 'messenger of God' or 'my strength is God'.
VARIANTS: Gab, Gabby, Gabi, Gabriele, Gabrielli, Gabriello, Gabris, Gay

Gael

This name has many possible sources: from the Old French for 'gallant', the Old English for 'lively', the Irish Gaelic for 'stranger' and the Old Welsh for 'wild'. Gael is also used as a male form of Gail, which is a short form of the Hebrew Abigail ('my father rejoices').
VARIANTS: Gail, Gaile, Gale, Gay, Gayle

Galvin

From the Gaelic for 'sparrow' or 'brilliant white'.
VARIANTS: Gal, Galvan, Galven

Gamal

An Arabic name meaning 'beauty'.
VARIANTS: Gamali, Gamli, Gil, Gilad, Gilead, Jammal

Ganesh

This is the name of the elephant-headed Hindu god and it means 'lord of the hosts' in Sanskrit.

Gareth

A name from Arthurian legend with Welsh roots, Gareth means 'gentle'.
VARIANTS: Garth, Gary, Garry

Garfield

From the Old English for a 'triangular piece of land', thus Garfield may have originally been used for someone who lived near a triangular field.
VARIANTS: Field, Gar, Gary

Gary

A short form of Gareth and Garfield.
VARIANTS: Gareth, Garfield, Gari, Garret, Garrett, Garry, Garth, Gaz

Gavin

An Arthurian name whose Welsh meaning is 'falcon' or 'hawk'.
VARIANTS: Gauvain, Gauvin, Gav, Gawain, Gawaine, Gawen

Gene

A short form of Eugene, which comes from the Greek for 'noble' or 'well-born'.
VARIANT: Eugene

Geoffrey

As a variant of Godfrey, this has the Germanic meaning 'God's peace'. It may also come from the German for 'territory' and 'stranger' or 'pledge', or from the Old German for 'peaceful traveller'.
VARIANTS: Geoff, Godfrey, Jeff, Jefferies, Jefferson, Jeffery, Jeffries

George

Despite being associated with men of great power, the name George comes from the Greek for 'farmer'.
VARIANTS: Geo, Georg, Georges, Georgie, Georgio, Georgy, Jorgen

Geraint

A popular Welsh name derived from the Greek for 'old man'.

Gerald

The Germanic name Gerald means 'spear rule'.
VARIANTS: Garald, Geraldo, Geralt, Gerard, Gerry, Jarrett, Jed, Jerald, Jerry

Gerard

A variant of Gerald, meaning 'spear rule'.
VARIANTS: Garrard, Gearad, Gerald, Geraldo, Gerhardt, Gerry, Jarrett, Jerald, Jerrard, Jerry

Gervase

Thought to mean 'spear' or 'armour bearer' in Old German or 'servant' in Celtic.
VARIANTS: Gervais, Gervaise, Gervasius, Gervis, Jarvis

Gideon

The Hebrew meaning of his name is 'maimed', 'stump' or 'powerful warrior'.
VARIANT: Gid

Gil

From the Hebrew for 'joy'. Also the short form of Gilbert, which comes from the Old German for 'bright hostage'.
VARIANTS: Gilbert, Gili, Gill, Gilli

Giles

A name of Greek origin meaning 'kid' or 'goatskin'. It may also come from the Scottish Gaelic for 'servant'.
VARIANTS: Gide, Gidie, Gile, Gilean, Gill, Gilles, Gyles

Gilmore

From the Old Norse for 'deep glen' and the Old English for 'tree root'.
VARIANTS: Gill, Gillie, Gillmore, Gilmour

Glen

A Scottish family name derived from the Gaelic word 'gleann', which means 'valley'.

Gordon

The Old English meaning of the first element 'gor' is 'marsh' and the Scottish Gaelic interpretation of the second part of the name is 'small wooded dell'.
VARIANTS: Goran, Gordan, Gorden, Gordie, Gordy, Gore

Grady

The Latin meaning of this name is 'step', 'position', 'degree' or 'grade'. It also comes from the Irish Gaelic for 'bright or exalted one'.
VARIANT: Gradey

Graham

An Old English place name which means 'gravel town', 'grey town', 'grant town' or, from Latin, 'grain town'.

Gram

A short form of Graham and also a pet form of Ingram, which is derived from the Old Norse for 'Ing's raven', Ing being the god of peace and fertility.
VARIANTS: Graham, Gramm, Ingram

Granger

From the Latin for 'grain', used to describe a person who worked on a farm.

Grant

Derived from the Old French 'granter', which means 'to agree, promise or bestow'.
VARIANTS: Grantland, Grantley

Gray

In Old English the name Gray means 'bailiff' or 'grey'.
VARIANTS: Greg, Grey, Greyson

Gregory

From the Greek meaning 'watchful' or 'be vigilant'.
VARIANT: Greg

Guy

Originally a short form of Guido, which is thought to come from the Old German for 'wide' or 'wood', or the Latin for 'lively'.
VARIANTS: Gui, Guido, Viti, Vitus

Gwyn

From the Welsh for 'blessed, holy' and 'white', Gwyn is the masculine equivalent of Gwen.
VARIANTS: Gwynfor, Wyn, Wynn, Wynford

Hal

The short form of various names, including Henry, Harry and Harold, all of which come from the Old German for 'army leader'.
VARIANTS: Hal, Haley, Halford, Halley, Hollis, Holly

Hale

From the Old English word 'hal', which means 'safe, sound, healthy and whole'.
VARIANTS: Hal, Haley, Halford, Halley, Harley, Hollis, Holly

Hamal

An Arabic name meaning 'lamb'.

Hamilton

From the Old English, meaning 'home' and 'lover' or 'blunt, flat-topped hill'.
VARIANTS: Hamel, Hamil, Hamill

Hamish

The Anglicised spelling of Seamus, which is the Gaelic version of James, and means 'supplanter' from the Hebrew.
VARIANTS: Jacob, James

Hank

A pet form of Henry, which means 'home ruler' in Old German.
VARIANTS: Hankin, Henry

Hans

The short form of Johannes, which is a German version of John.
VARIANTS: Johannes, John

Harding

Derived from the Old English meaning 'hardy, brave and strong'.
VARIANTS: Harden, Hardy

Hardy

From the Old French for 'to grow bold'. It is also used as a pet form of Harding.
VARIANTS: Harden, Hardie, Hardin, Harding

Harlan

Derived from the Old English for 'grey or hare land'.
VARIANTS: Harland, Harley

Harold

From both the Old English for 'army ruler' and the Old German name Heriwald, which means 'army power'.
VARIANTS: Hal, Haldon, Halford, Harald, Hariwald, Harlow, Harry

Harper

See *Harper* in the Girls' section.

Harrison

Harrison means simply 'son of Harry'.
VARIANTS: Harold, Harry

Harvey

Anglicised form of the French Hervé, which means 'battle-worthy'.
VARIANTS: Ervé, Harv, Harve, Harveson, Hervé, Hervey, Hervi

Hassan

This Arabic name means 'handsome', 'good' or 'pleasant'.
VARIANTS: Asan, Hasan

Haydn

Derived from the Old High German for 'heathen', but also from the Old English for 'hay' and 'grassy dell'.
VARIANTS: Hayden, Haydon, Hayes, Hays, Haywood, Heywood

Heath

An Old English name meaning 'from the heath'.

Hector

From the Greek for 'to restrain' or 'anchor'.
VARIANTS: Eachann, Eachdonn, Ector, Ettore, Heck, Heckie, Hecky

Henry

A name from the Old German meaning 'home ruler'.
VARIANTS: Enri, Enric, Enrico, Enrique, Hal, Hank, Harry, Heinrich, Heinz, Henri

Herbert

An Old French name of German (Frankish) origin, which means 'bright army'.
VARIANTS: Bert, Bertie, Herb, Herbie

Herman

The Old High German meaning of Herman is 'army man' or 'soldier'.
VARIANTS: Armand, Armant, Harman, Hermann, Hermie, Hermy

Hilal

An Arabic name which means 'new moon'.
VARIANT: Hilel

Hiram

The Hebrew meaning of Hiram is 'brother of the exalted one'.

Hoffman

A German name that means 'courtier' or 'man of influence and flattery'.

Holt

The Old English meaning of the name Holt is 'wooded hill' or 'copse'.

Homer

In Greek the name Homer means 'being hostage or led'. The Old French interpretation of the name is 'helmet maker' and it also comes from the Old English for 'pool in a hollow'.
VARIANTS: Homero, Omero

Howard

In English, Howard may come from the Old English for 'fence-keeper' or 'hog warden'. But it also has interpretations from Scandinavian ('high guardian') and Old German ('heart protector' and 'bold').
VARIANTS: Hogg, Howey, Howie, Ward

Hugh

The Old German meaning of Hugh is 'mind, spirit', but the Celtic Hu, or Hew, means 'fire' or 'inspiration'.
VARIANTS: Bert, Bertie, Berty, Hew, Hubert, Huey, Hughie, Hugo, Huw

Hugo

The German version of Hugh, meaning 'mind, spirit'.

Humphrey

This name comes from the Old German for 'strength' and 'peace'.
VARIANTS: Hum, Humfrey, Humfrid, Hump, Humph, Humphry

Hunter

First used in Scotland, Hunter comes from the Old English word 'huntian', which meant 'to search diligently, pursue or track down'. The Old Norse meaning of the name is 'to group'.
VARIANTS: Huntington, Huntley, Lee, Leigh

Huxley

The Old English meaning of Huxley is 'field of ash trees'.
VARIANTS: Haskell, Hux, Lee, Leigh

Hyam

The Jewish name Hyam comes from the Hebrew for 'life'.

Hywel

From the Welsh for 'eminent' or 'conspicuous' and the Old English for 'swine hill'.
VARIANTS: Howe, Howel, Howell, Howey, Howland

Iago
The Spanish and Welsh version of James, which means 'supplanter' in Hebrew.
VARIANTS: Jacob, James

Ian
The Scottish variant of John, which means 'God is gracious', 'God is merciful' and 'God has favoured' in Hebrew.
VARIANTS: Iain, John

Ibrahim
The Arabic form of Abraham, which means 'father of many' or 'father of a multitude'.
VARIANT: Abraham

Ieuan
A Welsh version of John, which means 'God is gracious', 'God is merciful' and 'God has favoured'.
VARIANTS: Iefan, Ifan

Ike
The short form of the Hebrew name Isaac, which means 'he laughed' or 'laughter'.
VARIANT: Isaac

Ingmar
Often found in Scandinavian countries, this comes from the Norse for 'famous son'.

Ingram
Ing was the Norse god of peace and fertility. The name Ingram comes from the Old Norse for 'Ing's raven'.
VARIANTS: Gram, Ingo, Ingrim

Innes
From the Gaelic for 'island'.
VARIANT: Innis

Iolo
This Welsh name is a short form of Iorwerth, which means 'lord', 'value' and 'worth'. It is also the Welsh equivalent of Edward.
VARIANT: Edward

Ira
An Old Testament name, which means 'leader'.

Irvin
From the Gaelic Irving, one meaning of which is 'handsome or fair', another is from the Welsh for 'green, fresh' or 'white water'. In Scotland it meant 'west river', while in Old English it pertained to 'sea' or 'boar and friend'.
VARIANTS: Irvine, Irving

Isaac
From the Hebrew meaning 'he laughed' or 'laughter'.
VARIANTS: Ike, Isaacus, Isaak, Isac, Itzik, Izaak

Ishmael
This biblical name means 'God hears' or 'outcast' in Hebrew.
VARIANTS: Esmael, Isamel, Ismael, Ysmael

Islwyn
A Welsh name that means 'below the grove'.

Israel
In Hebrew this name means either 'may God prevail' or 'he who strives with God'.

Ivan
The Slavic version John.
VARIANTS: Evo, Evon, Ivo, Vanya, Yvan, Yvon

Ivor
This name may come from the Latin for 'ivory' or the Welsh for 'lord' or 'archer'. Another possible source is the Old Norse for 'bow made of yew' or 'army'.
VARIANTS: Ifor, Iomhar, Ivair, Ivar, Ive, Iver, Ivon, Yvon

Jack

As a pet form of the name John ('God is gracious') or sometimes James ('supplanter').
VARIANTS: Jacob, Jacques, James, John

Jacob

From the Hebrew for 'follower' or 'supplanter'.
VARIANTS: Iago, Jack, Jacobson, Jacoby, Jacques, Jago, Jaime, Jakab, Jake, Jamie

Jago

A Cornish form of James.
VARIANTS: Iago, Jack, Jacobson, Jacoby, Jacques, Jaime, Jakab, Jake, James, Jamie

Jake

A pet form of the names John and Jacob.
VARIANTS: Jacob, Jacobson, Jacoby, Jacques, Jakab, James, Jamie, John

Jamal

An Arabic name meaning 'handsome'.
VARIANTS: Gamal, Jahmal, Jamaal, Jamael, Jamahl, Jamall, Jamel, Jameel, Jamil

James

Derived from the same Latin source as Jacob, James means 'supplanter'.
VARIANTS: Hamish, Jack, Jacob, Jacques, Jaime, Jamie, Jim, Jimmie, Jimmy, Seamus

Jared

The Hebrew meaning of Jared's name was 'descent'. The name also comes from the Greek for 'rose' and is a variant of Gerard, which means 'brave or strong spear'.
VARIANTS: Gerard, Jarett, Jarrad, Jarrath, Jarratt, Jarrod, Jered

Jarvis

This may come from the Germanic for 'spear', as a variant of Gerard. It may equally come from the Celtic for 'servant'.
VARIANTS: Gary, Gervais, Gervaise, Gervase, Jary, Jarry, Jerve, Jervis

Jason

A variant of the biblical name Joshua, Jason comes from the Hebrew 'God saves'. Its Greek meaning is 'to heal'.
VARIANTS: Jace, Jay, Joshua

Jasper

Derived from the Persian meaning 'treasurer', Jasper is also the name of a semi-precious stone.
VARIANTS: Caspar, Casper, Gaspar, Gaspard, Kasper

Jay

A short form of the biblical names James and Jacob, or a name derived from the Latin meaning 'chatterbox', like the bird.
VARIANTS: Jacob, James, Jaye, Jey, Jeye

Jed

Originally used as a short form of the Hebrew Jedidiah, 'beloved of God'.
VARIANTS: Jedd, Jedidiah

Jefferson

Jefferson simply means 'son of Jeffrey'.

Jenson

'Son of Johannes' in Danish.
VARIANTS: Jensen, Jenssen

Jeremy

Derived from the biblical name Jeremiah, which means 'appointed or exalted by God'.
VARIANTS: Gerome, Gerrie, Gerry, Jem, Jeremiah, Jerome, Jerry

Jermaine

A variant of Germaine, from the Latin for 'clan brother'.
VARIANTS: Germain, Germaine, Germane, Germayne, Jermain, Jermayn, Jerri, Jerrie, Jerry

Jerome

A variant of Gerome, from the Greek for 'holy and sacred name'.
VARIANTS: Gerome, Geronimus, Gerrie, Gerry, Jeromo, Jerrome, Jerry

Jesse

A Hebrew name meaning 'gift'.
VARIANTS: Jake, Jess, Jessie, Jessy

Jesus

A variant of Joshua, which comes from the Hebrew for 'God saves' or 'the Lord is my salvation'.
VARIANTS: Hesus, Jesous, Jesu, Jesuso, Jezus, Joshua

Jet

A short form of Jethro, from the Hebrew for 'excellence' or 'wealth'. It also means 'stone'.
VARIANTS: Jethro, Jett

Jethro

A Biblical name meaning 'excellence' or 'wealth'.
VARIANTS: Jet, Jeth, Jett

Job

This biblical name, associated with great patience, means 'persecuted' or 'oppressed' in Hebrew.
VARIANTS: Joabee, Joabie, Jobey, Jobie, Joby

Jock

The Scottish variant of Jack and John.
VARIANTS: Jack, John

Joel

The Hebrew meaning of Joel is 'Jehovah is God' and 'God is willing'.
VARIANT: Yoel

John

This very popular biblical name comes from the Hebrew for 'God is gracious', 'God is merciful' and 'God has favoured'.
VARIANTS: Ian, Ivan, Jack, Jock, Johannes, Jonnie, Jonny, Juan, Owen, Zane

Jonah

From the Hebrew for 'dove' or 'pigeon'.
VARIANTS: Jonas, Yona, Yonah

Jonathan

A name from the Old Testament that means 'God's gift'.
VARIANTS: Johnathan, Johnathon, Jon, Jonathon, Jonnie, Jonny, Jonty, Yonatan

Jordan

The name of a holy river, from the Hebrew for 'to flow down'.
VARIANTS: Jared, Jarrod, Jerad, Jordain, Jori, Jory, Judd

Joseph

The Hebrew meaning of Joseph is 'God will add (another son)'.
VARIANTS: Jo, Joe, Joey, Jojo, José, Josephe, Yousef

Joshua

The Hebrew meaning of Joshua is 'the Lord saves'.
VARIANTS: Hosea, Jason, Jesous, Jesus, Josh

Juan

Juan is the Spanish version of John.
VARIANTS: DeJuan, John

Judd

As a variant of Jordan, Judd comes from the Hebrew for 'to flow down', but as a short form of Judah it means 'praise'.
VARIANTS: Jordan, Judah, Jude

Jude

Like Judd, Jude is derived from Judah, which means 'praise' in Hebrew.
VARIANTS: Jud, Juda, Judah, Judas, Judd, Judson, Yehudi

Julian

Thought to come from the Latin for 'fair-skinned'.
VARIANTS: Giuliano, Iola, Jolin, Jolyon, Jule, Jules, Julianus, Julius, Julyan

Justin

From the Latin for 'just' or 'fair'.
VARIANTS: Iestin, Iestyn, Justinian, Justis, Justus, Jut

Kalil

From the Arabic for 'good friend', the Greek for 'beautiful' or the Hebrew for 'wealth' or 'crown'.
VARIANTS: Kahil, Kahlil, Kailil, Kal, Kallie, Khaleel, Khalil

Kalle

The Scandinavian meaning of this name is 'strong' and 'manly'.

Kamal

From the Arabic for 'perfection'. In India it is the name for the lotus flower and comes from the Sanskrit for 'pale red'.
VARIANTS: Kameel, Kamil

Kane

The Anglicised form of the Irish Gaelic name Cathan, which means 'warrior'. Kane also comes from the Celtic for 'tribute', 'battler' and 'dark'. The Welsh meaning of Kane is 'lovely'. In Japan it means 'golden' and the Hawaiian interpretation is 'man'. It may also come from the Old French for 'battlefield'.
VARIANTS: Kain, Kaine, Kayne

Karim

From the Arabic for 'generous' and 'noble'.
VARIANTS: Kareem, Kario

Kasimir

The Slavonic meaning of Kasimir is 'commands peace', or, alternatively, 'to spoil peace'.

Kasper

The German form of Jasper, which comes from the Persian for 'treasurer'.
VARIANTS: Caspar, Casper, Gaspar, Gaspard, Jasper, Kaspa

Kayden

From the Old English 'cade', meaning 'cask' or 'companion'.
VARIANTS: Caden, Kaden'

Keane

The Irish Gaelic meaning of Keane is 'warrior's son'. In Old English, the name means 'wise, clever' or 'brave and strong'. It is also the Anglicised form of the Gaelic name Cian, which means 'ancient'.
VARIANTS: Kane, Kani, Kayne, Kean, Keen, Keenan, Keene, Kene, Kian, Kienan

Keir

The Irish Gaelic meaning of Keir is 'dark-skinned' or 'spear', although it also has an Old Norse meaning – 'marshland containing brushwood'.
VARIANT: Kerr

Keith

A Scottish name with the Gaelic meaning 'wood', or 'battlefield' in Irish Gaelic.

Kelly

See *Kelly* in the Girls' section.

Kelsey

From the Irish Gaelic for 'warrior', but can also derive from 'ship's keel' or 'ship' and 'victory'.
VARIANTS: Kelcey, Kelley, Kelsee, Kelsie, Kelson, Kelton

Kelvin

The Old English meaning of Kelvin is 'ship's keel' or 'friend'. It also means 'narrow stream' in Gaelic.
VARIANTS: Kelvan, Kelven, Kelwin

Kendall

A name of Old English origin, meaning 'royal valley'. It also has Celtic origins, meaning 'high, exalted' and 'image, effigy'.
VARIANTS: Ken, Kendahl, Kendal, Kendale, Kendell, Kendyl, Kenn, Kennie, Kenny, Kyndal

Kennedy

From the Irish Gaelic for 'head' and 'ugly'. It also comes from the Old English for 'ruler'.
VARIANTS: Ken, Kenman, Kenn, Kennard, Kennie, Kenny, Kent, Kenton, Kenyan

Kenneth

The Gaelic meaning of the name Kenneth is either 'born of fire' or 'handsome'. The Old English meaning is 'royal oath'.
VARIANTS: Cainnech, Ken, Kene, Kenn, Kennie, Kenny, Kent, Kenton, Kenward

Kent

The name of an English county and also a short form of the name Kenton, which may come from the Old English for 'royal manor'. As a derivative of Kenneth it means 'born of fire', 'handsome' or 'royal oath'.
VARIANTS: Ken, Kennedy, Kenneth, Kenton, Kenyon

Kern

The Old Irish meaning of Kern is 'band of infantry'.
VARIANTS: Kearney, Kearny

Kerry

See *Kerry* in the Girls' section.

Kevin

Kevin is derived from an Old Irish name that means 'handsome birth'.
VARIANTS: Coemgen, Kerrie, Kerry, Kev, Kevan, Keven

Kieran

Like the girl's name Kiera, Kieran comes from the Irish word 'ciar', which means 'black', hence 'dark one'.
VARIANTS: Ciaran, Ciaren, Kiaran, Kyron

Killian

An Irish saint's name, derived from either the word for 'strife', or 'church', or 'little warrior'.
VARIANTS: Cilian, Cillian, Killie, Killy, Kilmer

Kim

The Greek meaning of Kim is 'hollow vessel', but it also comes from the Old English for 'kin' or 'royal' and 'bold'. In Welsh the name means 'chief' and 'war'.
VARIANTS: Kimball, Kimberley, Kimberly

Kingsley

The Old English meaning of this name is 'king's clearing' or 'king's wood'.
VARIANTS: King, Kingsleigh, Kingsly, Kingston, Kinsey

Kirk

This has roots in Old English, Scottish and Scandinavian, and means 'church' in all three languages.
VARIANTS: Kerk, Kirby, Kirke, Kirklan, Kirkland, Kirtland, Kyrk

Klaus

See *Claus* and *Nicholas*.

Kumar

From the Sanskrit for 'prince' or 'son'.

Kurt

As the short form of Conrad, Kurt comes from the German for 'brave advice' or 'bold, wise counsellor'.
VARIANTS: Conrad, Curt, Curtis, Kurtis

Kushal

An Indian name that means 'clever'.

Kyle

A Scottish place name that comes from the Gaelic for 'narrow strait'.
VARIANTS: Kile, Ky

Lachlan

In Scotland Lachlan was the Gaelic name given to someone from Norway. It means 'from the land of the lakes' or 'warlike'.
VARIANTS: Lachann, Lachie, Lachlann

Lal

From the Sanskrit for 'caress' and the Hindi for 'beloved'.

Lamar

A surname and a first name, Lamar comes from the French for 'the pond'.

Lambert

From the Old High German for 'bright or shining land'. It also means 'pride of the nation'.
VARIANTS: Bert, Bertie, Berty, Lamberto, Lammie, Landbert

Lamont

From the Norse for 'law man' and the Scottish Gaelic for 'law giver'. It also comes from the French meaning 'the mountain'.
VARIANTS: Lamond, Lammond, LaMont, Lemont, Monty

Lance

Originally a name given to somebody who carried a lance in battle.
VARIANTS: Lancelot, Lancing, Lansing, Launce, Launcelot

Lawrence

The Latin meaning of Lawrence is 'from Laurentum', Laurentum being the Roman name of an Italian town.
VARIANTS: Larrance, Larry, Lars, Larse, Larson, Laurel, Laurence, Laurent, Lorenzo, Lowrie

Leander

Derived from two Greek words 'leon', which means 'lion', and 'andros', which means 'man'. Thus it means 'lion man'.
VARIANTS: Ander, Andor, Lea, Leandre, Leandro, Lee, Leo, Leon, Maclean

Lee

Derived from the Old English word 'leah', which means 'wood, clearing' or 'meadow'.
VARIANTS: Lea, Leigh

Lennox

Originally a place name in Scotland, this comes from the Scottish Gaelic for 'elms' and 'water'.

Leo

From the Latin for 'lion'.
VARIANTS: Leander, Lee, Leon, Leonardo, Leopold, Lonnie

Leonard

From the Old High German for 'strong as a lion' or 'lion' and 'hard'.
VARIANTS: Lenard, Lenn, Lennard, Lenny, Leo, Leon, Leonardo, Lionardo, Lonnie

Leroy

Derived from French, meaning 'the king'.
VARIANTS: Elroy, Lee, Lee Roy, Roy

Leslie

See *Lesley* in the Girls' section.

Lester

A contracted form of Leicester, which is a town in England, whose name meant 'Roman clearing' or 'Roman fort' in Old English.
VARIANTS: Leicester, Les, Letcher, Leycester

Levi

The Hebrew meaning of this Old Testament name is 'attached' or 'pledged'.
VARIANTS: Lavey, Lavi, Lavy, Leavitt, Lev, Levey, Levy

Lex

As a pet form of Alexander, Lex comes from the Greek for 'defender of men' or 'warrior'. It may also be derived from the Latin word for 'law'.
VARIANTS: Alexander, Laxton, Lexie, Lexton

Liam

The short form of the Gaelic version of William, which means 'resolute protection'. It also comes from the French for 'to bind' or 'protect'.
VARIANTS: Lyam, William

Linden

The Old English meaning of Linden is 'lime tree' or 'the hill with linden trees'.
VARIANTS: Lin, Lindon, Lindy, Lyn, Lynden, Lyndon, Lynn

Lindsay

See *Lindsey* in the Girls' section.

Lionel

A name connected with Arthurian legend, derived from the French meaning 'little lion'.
VARIANTS: Len, Lennie, Lenny, Leo, Leon, Leonel, Lionell, Lonnell

Lewis

The Old Germanic meaning of Lewis is 'famous warrior' or 'famous battle'.
VARIANTS: Lew, Lewie, Louis, Ludwig

Llewellyn

A Welsh name which means 'leader', 'lion' and 'resemblance'.
VARIANTS: Fluellen, Llywellwyn, Lywelyn, Lyn

Lloyd

From the Welsh for 'brown, grey', used for a person's complexion or hair colour.
VARIANTS: Floyd, Llwyd, Loy, Loyd

Logan

Derived from Scottish and Irish place names that mean 'little hollow', Logan could also be an occupational name, from the Middle English word 'logge', which means 'record or journal of performance'.

Lorenzo

The Italian and Spanish form of Lawrence.
VARIANTS: Laurence, Lawrence, Loren

Lorimer

A name of Latin origin meaning 'harness maker'.
VARIANTS: Lori, Lorrie, Lorry

Louis

A French variant of Lewis, meaning 'famous battle or warrior'.
VARIANTS: Aloysius, Clovis, Elois, Lewie, Lewis, Ludvig, Ludwig, Luis

Lucas

From the Greek for 'from Luciana', a region in southern Italy.
VARIANTS: Luc, Lucais, Luka, Lukas, Luke

Ludovic

Like Lewis and Louis, Ludovic comes from the German for 'famed warrior' or 'famous battle'. It can also be a derivation of the Gaelic for 'devotee of the Lord'.
VARIANTS: Lewis, Louis, Ludo, Ludovick, Ludwig

Luke

Like Lucas, Luke comes from the Greek for 'from Luciana'.
VARIANTS: Luc, Lucais, Luka, Lukas

Luther

From the Old German for 'people' and 'army'.
VARIANTS: Lothar, Lothario, Lother, Lutero

Mace
Of Latin origin referring to the aromatic spice of the same name.
VARIANTS: Maceo, Macey, Mack, Mackey, Macy

Maddox
Both Celtic and English in origin, Maddox means 'son of the Lord' and 'beneficent'.

Madison
Originally a surname, Madison comes from the Old English for 'son of Maud', 'son of Matthew' or 'son of Magdalene'.
VARIANTS: Maddi, Maddie, Maddison, Maddy

Magnus
From the Latin meaning 'great'.
VARIANT: Manus

Malachai
A Hebrew name meaning 'my messenger' or 'my angel'.
VARIANTS: Mal, Malachy

Malcolm
The name Malcolm means 'devotee or servant of Columba'.
VARIANTS: Colm, Colum, Mal, Maolcolm

Malik
An Arabic name meaning 'master'.
VARIANTS: Mal, Mali

Manfred
This comes from the Old German for 'man of peace'.
VARIANTS: Fred, Freddie, Freddy, Manifred, Mannie, Manny, Mannye

Mansur
An Arabic name, which means 'divinely helped' or 'helped by God'.

Mark
Possibly from the Latin for 'martial', as a derivative of Mars, the god of war.
VARIANTS: Marc, Marcel, Marcello, Marco, Marcus, Marques, Marquis, Mars

Marley
More common as a surname, Marley means 'field near water'.

Marlon
As a variant of Marlow, this may come from the Old English for 'pond', 'sea' and 'remnant'. But it may equally be derived from the Welsh for 'sea' and 'hill' or 'fort', as a variant of Merlin.
VARIANTS: Mar, Mario, Marle, Marlen, Marlin, Marlo, Marlow, Marlowe, Merlin

Marlow
From the Old English for 'pond', 'sea' and 'remnant'.
VARIANTS: Marle, Marlin, Marlis, Marlon

Marshall
The transferred use of an Old French occupational surname – either someone who looked after horses or a high-ranking official in the royal household.
VARIANTS: Marsh, Marshal, Marshe

Martin
Like Mark, this is thought to come from the Latin Mars, the Roman god of war.
VARIANTS: Mart, Martainn, Martel, Marten, Martie, Martyn

Marvin
The Old English meaning of Marvin is 'famous friend'. As a variant of Mervyn it means 'sea fort'.
VARIANTS: Marv, Marve, Marven, Marvine, Marvyn, Mervyn, Merwin, Merwyn

Maskil
The Hebrew meaning of Maskil is 'educated' or 'learned'.

Mason
An occupational name for someone who works with stone.

Matthew
The Hebrew meaning of Matthew is 'gift of God'.
VARIANTS: Macey, Mat, Mate, Mateus, Matiah, Matias, Matt, Mattie, Matty

Maurice

From the Latin name 'Maurus', which was used for the North African Moorish race.
VARIANTS: Maryse, Maur, Maurie, Morey, Morie, Morris, Morry, Morus

Max

A short form of Maximilian, from the Latin for 'great', and also of Maxwell, which is of Scottish origin meaning 'Mac's well'.
VARIANTS: Mac, Mack, Maks, Massimo, Maxey, Maxie, Maxim, Maximilian, Maxwell

Maxwell

Originally a Scottish surname that means 'Mac's well'.
VARIANTS: Mac, Mack, Maks, Max, Maxie, Maxim, Maxime, Maxy

Melvin

From the Old English for 'council' and 'friend', or the German for 'Amalo's settlement'. As a variant of Melville, it has the Old French meaning 'bad town'.
VARIANTS: Mel, Melville, Melvyn

Michael

The biblical name Michael means 'who is like God' in Hebrew.
VARIANTS: Michele, Mick, Mickey, Miguel, Mikael, Mike, Misha, Mitchell, Mychal

Milan

A Czech name that means 'grace', and also the name of an Italian city.

Miles

Possibly a variant of the biblical name Michael, or from the Latin for 'mils' of a thousand (mills) paces, or the Old German for 'beloved' or 'gentle'.
VARIANTS: Michael, Milan, Mills, Milo, Myles

Milo

From the Old Slavic for 'grace' and the Germanic for 'merciful'.
VARIANTS: Miles, Myles

Milton

The Old English meaning of the name Milton is 'mill town' or 'middle settlement'.
VARIANTS: Millard, Miller, Mills, Milt, Miltie, Milty, Mull, Muller

Mitchell

A variant of the biblical name Michael, meaning 'who is like God'.
VARIANTS: Michael, Mitch, Mitchel

Monty

Short for Montgomery, which comes from the French for 'mountain' and a German personal name that means 'power of man'. It is also a variant of Montague, which comes from the French and Latin for 'pointed mountain' or 'big hill'.
VARIANTS: Montague, Monte, Montgomerie, Montgomery

Morgan

See *Morgan* in the Girls' section.

Mortimer

An aristocratic surname taken from the French place name 'mort mer', which means 'dead sea'.
VARIANTS: Mort, Mortie, Morty

Moses

An Old Testament name whose Hebrew meaning is 'saved from the water'.
VARIANTS: Moe, Moke, Mosheh, Moss, Moy, Moyes, Moyse

Muhammad

The name of the prophet who founded Islam, Muhammad means 'praised' or 'glorified' in Arabic.

VARIANTS: Mahamet, Mohamad, Mohamed, Mohammad, Mohammed

Murdoch

From the Irish and Scottish Gaelic for 'sailor' or 'seaman'.

VARIANTS: Murdo, Murdock, Murtagh, Murtaugh

Murray

From the Scottish district of Moray, which takes its name from the Old Celtic for 'settlement by the sea'.

VARIANTS: Murrie, Murry

Naaman
Taken from the Hebrew for 'beautiful, pleasant' or the Arabic 'good fortune'.

Naim
Derived from the Arabic for 'comfortable' or 'contented'.
VARIANT: Naeem

Namid
A name from Native American legend, which means 'star dancer'.

Namir
An Arabic name meaning 'leopard'.

Naresh
From the Sanskrit for 'lord' or 'king'.

Nassar
An Arabic name meaning of Nassar is 'victorious'.

Nathan
In Hebrew Nathan means 'gift'. It is also a short form of Jonathan and Nathaniel, both of which mean 'God's gift'.
VARIANTS: Jonathan, Jonathon, Nat, Nata, Natan, Nate, Nathaniel

Nathaniel
Nathaniel was one of Christ's Apostles whose name comes from the Hebrew for 'he gave' or 'God's gift'.
VARIANTS: Nat, Nata, Natal, Natale, Natan, Natanael, Nathan

Nav
An English gypsy name which means simply 'name'.
VARIANT: Nev

Ned

A short form of Edward, derived from the Old English for 'happiness, riches' and 'guardian'.
VARIANTS: Edmund, Edward, Neddie, Neddy, Ted, Teddie, Teddy

Neil

The Anglicised form of the Gaelic name Niall, which means 'cloud', 'passionate' and 'champion'.
VARIANTS: Neal, Neale, Neall, Nealson, Neely, Neill, Nelson, Niall, Nyles

Nelson

A name associated with great leaders, Nelson means simply 'son of Neil'.
VARIANTS: Nealson, Neaton, Neil, Nils, Nilsen, Nilson

Nemo

A short form of Nahum, which comes from the Hebrew for 'comforting'. Its Greek meaning is 'from the glen'.
VARIANT: Nahum

Neville

Originally a surname, Neville comes from the French for 'new town'.
VARIANTS: Nev, Nevil, Nevile, Nevill

Newton

Like Neville, Newton means 'new town or settlement'.
VARIANTS: Newgate, Newland, Newman, Newt

Niall

An Irish and Scottish Gaelic name which means 'cloud', 'passionate' and 'champion'.
VARIANTS: Neil, Nelson

Nicholas

From the Greek for 'victorious people'.
VARIANTS: Claus, Klaas, Klaus, Nic, Niccolo, Nick, Nicky, Nicolai

Nigel

A Latinised form of the Irish Gaelic name Niall, meaning 'champion', 'passionate' and 'cloud'. Also derived from the Old Latin for 'dark, night'.
VARIANTS: Neil, Nidge, Nige, Nigi, Niguel, Nye

Nir

From the Hebrew for 'ploughed field' and associated with industry and fruitfulness.
VARIANTS: Niral, Nirel, Niria

Noam

From the Hebrew for 'joy, delight and pleasantness'.

Noble

From the Latin word 'nobilis', which means 'renowned, famous' or 'born into nobility'.

Noel

The Old French word for 'birthday of the Lord', traditionally given to babies born at Christmas.
VARIANTS: Noël, Noëlle, Noelle

Nolan

An Irish family name that comes from the Irish Gaelic for 'famous noble' or 'son of the famous one'.
VARIANT: Noland

Norman

The Old English meaning of the name Norman was 'man from the north'.
VARIANTS: Norm, Normand, Normann, Normie

Nye

A pet form of the Welsh Aneurin, which means 'little one of pure gold', also derived from the Latin meaning 'man of honour'.
VARIANTS: Aneurin, Ny, Nyle

Oberon
A variant of Auberon, thought to be of German Frankish origin, meaning 'noble' and 'bear'.

Olaf
From the Old Norse meaning 'ancestor' or 'remains'.
VARIANTS: Olav, Olave, Ole, Olen, Olif

Oliver
An Old Norse name, taken from the French for 'olive tree'.
VARIANTS: Olivero, Olivier, Ollie

Omar
Arabic in origin, Omar has the meaning 'long life', 'flourishing', 'first-born son' and 'follower of the Prophet'.
VARIANTS: Omri, Oner

Orrin
From the Hebrew word for 'tree', or a variant of the Irish name Oran, meaning 'grey-brown' or 'dark'.
VARIANTS: Oren, Orin, Orren

Orson
From the old French for 'bear cub'.
VARIANTS: Sonnie, Sonny, Urson

Oscar
An old Norse name, Oscar means 'divine spear'.
VARIANTS: Ossie, Ossy

Ossian
A name of Irish derivation meaning 'little deer'.

Oswald
From the old English and Norse words for 'god and ruler' and 'power of wood'.
VARIANTS: Ossie, Osvald, Oswal, Oswaldo, Oswall, Oswold, Oz, Ozzie, Ozzy, Waldo, Waldy

Otis
Originating from the Greek for ear, as in giving and taking advice.
VARIANTS: Otes, Otto

Otto
From the German for 'wealth' and 'prosperity'.
VARIANTS: Odo, Osman, Othello, Othman, Othmar

Owen
The Welsh form of 'Eugene', Owen is derived from the Greek for 'well-born' or 'lucky'.
VARIANTS: Bowen, Bowie, Eoghan, Eugene, Euan, Evan, Ewen, Owain, Owayne, Ovin

Pablo

The Spanish version of Paul, derived from the Greek for 'small'.

Paddy

A pet form of Patrick, from the Latin meaning 'patrician' or a 'member of the Roman nobility'.

Paolo

The Italian version of Paul, from the Greek for 'small'.

Paris

Originating from the Latin name for the Gaulish Celtic tribe the Parisii. Also the name of the Trojan prince who abducted Helen of Troy and caused the Trojan War.

Parker

From the old French for 'park-keeper'.

Parley

Derived from the Latin word for 'discourse'.

Pascal

Derived from the Old French word for Easter.
VARIANTS: Pasco, Pascoe, Pasqual, Pesach

Patrick

From the Latin meaning 'patrician' or a 'member of the Roman nobility', Patrick is the patron saint of Ireland.
VARIANTS: Pad, Paddie, Paddy, Padriac, Pat, Patraic, Patric, Paxton

Paul

Derived from the Greek for 'small', the name Paul was borne by numerous saints.
VARIANTS: Pablo, Pal, Paolo, Pasha, Paulie, Paulino, Paulinus, Paulis, Paulo, Pol

Paxton

Derived from two Latin words, 'pax', meaning peace and 'tun', meaning 'town', hence the meaning 'town of peace'.

Penn

Meaning 'hill' in old English, 'commander' in ancient German and 'pen' or 'quill' in Latin, Penn first appeared as an Old English surname given to someone who lived near a sheep pen.
VARIANTS: Pennie, Penny, Penrod

Perry

From the Old English for 'pear tree', or a pet form of Peregrine, meaning 'foreigner or stranger', or a diminutive of Peter, meaning 'rock'.
VARIANT: Perigrine

Peter

Taken from the Greek for 'rock'.
VARIANTS: Perry, Pete, Pierre, Piers, Rock, Rocky

Philip

Originally from the Greek for 'loving horses'.
VARIANTS: Felip, Phil, Phillip, Philipot, Philippe, Pip

Phoenix

See *Phoenix* in Girls' section.

Piers

A French version of Peter, meaning 'rock'.

Pip

A diminutive of Philip.

Poco

An Italian name meaning 'little'.

Porter

Taken from the French for a 'door' or 'gate', the name Porter was initially bestowed upon someone who guarded a gate.

Powell

A derivation of Howell, taken from the Old English meaning 'wild boar or pig' and 'hill'.

Pravin

A Hindu name meaning 'skilful' or 'able'.

Preston

Initially a surname, Preston probably derives from the Old English for 'priest's town'.
VARIANT: Prescott

Purnal

Taken from the Latin, meaning 'pear', the purnal is a long-living tree, and a symbol of longevity in China.

Quincy

A French noble name, Quincy comes from the Latin for 'fifth'.
VARIANTS: Quentin, Quincey, Quintus

Quinn

The Irish meaning of Quinn is 'descendant of Conn' – Conn meaning 'leader' or 'chief'.
VARIANTS: Quentin, Quincy

Rabi
Arabic in origin, this name means 'fragrant breeze.'

Rafferty
Deriving from Gaelic and German roots, Rafferty means 'rich and prosperous.'
VARIANTS: Rafe, Rafer, Raff, Raffer

Raja
Arabic for 'anticipated' or 'hoped for'. It is the male version of Rani and means 'prince'.
VARIANT: Raj

Raleigh
An Old English name that comes from 'Ra', or 'roe deer', and 'leah' or 'grassy clearing'.

Ralph
From the Germanic for 'counsel' or 'might' (as in strength) and 'wolf'.
VARIANTS: Raaf, Rafe, Raff, Raffy, Randolph, Ranulf, Rauf, Rauffe, Rolf

Ramsey
Originating in the Old English meaning 'land of the rams'.
VARIANT: Ramsay

Randall
A version of Randolph, which is also a surname. (See *Randolph*.)
VARIANTS: Rand, Randal, Randel, Randl, Randle, Rands

Randolph
From the Old English for 'shield' and 'wolf', meaning 'brave protector'.
VARIANTS: Dolph, Rand, Randal, Randall, Randle, Randolf, Rands, Randy, Ranulf

Raphael
The name of an archangel in the Bible, Raphael comes from the Hebrew for 'God has healed'.
VARIANTS: Raf, Rafael, Rafaelle, Rafe, Rafel, Raffael, Raphel

Rashad
Of Arabic origin, Rashad means 'to have good sense' or 'integrity'.

Raul
From the Germanic for 'counsel' or 'might' (as in strength) and 'wolf', where it is a variant of Ralph.
VARIANTS: Ralph, Raolin, Raoul

Ravi
In Hindu mythology Ravi is the name of the sun god.

Ravid
A Hebrew name meaning 'jewellery' or 'adornment'.

Raymond
With its origins in Old German, Raymond means 'wise advisor or protector'.
VARIANTS: Monchi, Mondo, Mundo, Rai, Raimond, Ramond, Ramone, Ray, Raynard, Redmond

Redford
Taken from the Old English words 'red', meaning 'reedy', and 'ford', a shallow river crossing.
VARIANTS: Ford, Red, Redd

Reeves
Derived from the Old English for a bailiff, overseer or chief magistrate.
VARIANTS: Reave, Reeve

Regan
Derived from Hebrew and Old German roots, meaning 'wise'.
VARIANTS: Reagan, Reagen

René

A French name meaning 'reborn'.
VARIANTS: Renato, Renatus, Reni

Reuben

A biblical name, meaning 'behold, a son'.
VARIANTS: Rube, Ruben

Rex

A diminutive of Reginald and Reynold, Rex is Latin for 'ruler' or 'leader'.
VARIANTS: Ray, Rayner, Regino, Regis, Rexer, Rexford, Reynaud, Reyner

Rhodric

An Anglicised version of the Spanish Rodrigo, Rhodric comes from the Old German meaning 'famous ruler'.
VARIANTS: Revie, Ribbans, Rod, Rodd, Roddie, Roddy, Roderich, Roderick, Roderigo, Rodrich, Rodrique, Rofi, Rory, Rouven, Rouvin, Rube, Ruben, Rubens, Rubin, Ruby, Rurih, Ruvane, Ruvim, Ruy

Rhys

Derived from the Welsh word for 'ardour'.
VARIANTS: Ray, Reece, Rees, Reese, Rey, Rhett, Rice, Royce

Richard

Taken from the Germanic words meaning 'he who rules' and 'hard'.
VARIANTS: Dic, Dick, Dickie, Dicky, Ric, Ricard, Ricardo, Riccardo, Richey, Richie, Ritchie

Rider

A Middle English name, derived from the word 'ridde', meaning 'to clear' or 'to make space'.
VARIANTS: Rid, Riddle, Ridgeley, Ridley, Ryder, Ryerson

Riley

Taken from the Old English, meaning 'rye meadow'.
VARIANTS: Reilly, Royley, Ryley

Riordan

Of German and Gaelic origins, Riordan is derived from the words for 'royal' and 'poet'.
VARIANTS: Rearden, Riorden

Ripley

From the Old English for 'one who would clear wooded areas'.
VARIANTS: Lee, Leigh, Rip, Ripp

Robert

Derived from the ancient German for 'bright' and 'famous'.
VARIANTS: Bert, Bertie, Bob, Bobbie, Hobson, Robb, Robbie, Robby, Roberto, Robertson, Rory

Robin

The original French version of Robert.
VARIANTS: Rob, Robyn

Rockwell

The literal meaning is 'a well with rocks'.
VARIANTS: Roache, Rocco, Roch, Roche, Rocher, Rochie, Rochy

Rodney

Derived from Old English, meaning 'island of reeds'.
VARIANTS: Rod, Rodd, Roddie, Roddy

Roger

From the English 'hodge', meaning 'a peasant labourer', or from the German 'hrod', meaning 'fame', and 'ger', meaning 'spear'.

VARIANTS: Dodge, Hodge, Rodge, Rodger, Rog, Rogello, Rogerio, Rogers, Roggie, Roj, Rugero, Ruggerio, Rutger

Roland

From the Old German words for 'fame' and 'land'.

VARIANTS: Orlando, Rollie, Rolly, Roly, Rory, Rowles

Rolf

German in origin, Rolf means 'renowned for bravery'.

VARIANTS: Ralf, Rolfe, Rollo, Rolph, Rolphe, Roul, Roulf, Rudolf, Rudolph

Rollo

A variant of Roland and diminutive of Raoul, Rollo is believed to be the Old French version of Rolf.

VARIANTS: Rolan, Rolf, Rolly, Roul, Rudolf, Rudolph

Romain

With its literal meaning 'a citizen of Rome', Romain is essentially French for 'Roman'.

VARIANTS: Roman, Romano, Romeo, Romulus

Romeo

The romantic name Romeo comes from the Latin for 'Citizen of Rome'.

VARIANTS: Romallus, Roman, Romanus

Rory

Originally a nickname, Rory is the Anglicised version of a Gaelic name meaning 'red-haired one'.

VARIANTS: Roderick, Rorie, Rurik

Ross

A Gaelic name meaning 'headland', popular as a Scottish surname.

Roswell

Derived from the Old German, meaning 'a skilled fighting horseman'.

Rouel

A Hebrew name meaning 'friend of God'.

VARIANT: Ruel

Rowan

Of Gaelic origins, Rowan means 'red-haired' or 'rugged'.

VARIANTS: Rooney, Rouan, Rowan, Rowanne, Rowen, Rowney

Roy

With its origins in Gaelic, Roy means 'red'. Originally a reference to hair colour.

VARIANTS: Delroy, Elroy, Leroy, Loe, Ray, Rey, Roi, Royce, Royle, Royston

Rudy

A Germanic diminutive form of Rudolph and Rolf, meaning 'renowned for courage'.

Rudyard

An Old English name meaning 'red gate'.

Rufus

Of Latin derivation, meaning the 'red-haired one'.

Rupert

A development of the German name Rupprecht, meaning 'bright' and 'fame'.

VARIANTS: Robert, Rubert, Ruberto, Rudbert, Rupe, Ruperto, Rupprecht

Russell

Derived from the Old French for 'red-haired' or 'red-faced'.

VARIANTS: Rosario, Rus, Russ, Russel, Rustie, Rustin, Rusty

Ryan

The name Ryan has Gaelic origins and means 'little king'.

Samir
Arabic for 'entertainment'.
VARIANTS: Sameer, Zamir

Samson
Taken from the Hebrew meaning 'bright as the sun'.
VARIANTS: Sam, Sammy, Sampson, Shimson

Samuel
A biblical name of Hebrew origin, Samuel means 'asked of God' and may be a derivative of Saul.
VARIANTS: Sam, Sammie, Sammy, Shmuel

Sancho
A derivative of the Spanish for 'sincere' and 'thoughtful', as well as the Latin 'San Etus' meaning 'holy' and/or 'pure'.
VARIANT: Sanchez

Sasha
Originating in Old French, Sasha means 'defender' or 'helper' as in the 'helper of mankind'.
VARIANT: Sacha

Saul
From the Hebrew for 'asked/prayed for', as in a prayed-for child.
VARIANTS: Paul, Saulo, Shane, Shaul, Sol, Sollie, Solly

Sawyer
An occupational name meaning 'someone who saws'.
VARIANTS: Saw, Sawyere.

Scott
From the Latin nickname 'Scotti' for the Irish invaders who settled the west of Scotland.
VARIANT: Scot

Sean
The Irish version of John, meaning 'God is gracious'.
VARIANTS: Shaughan, Shane, Shaun

Sebastian
Derived from the Greek for 'venerable'.
VARIANTS: Bart, Bartiana, Barties, Bastian, Seb, Sebastianus, Sebbie

Seth
A Hebrew name meaning 'the appointed one'. In Sanskrit it also means 'bridge'.

Seymour
Derived from the old French place name of Saint-Maur, Maur meaning 'Moorish' or 'African'. In Old English the name is a combination of 'sae', meaning 'sea', and 'mor', meaning marshland or moor.
VARIANT: Seymore

Shaanan
Derived from the Hebrew word for 'peaceful'.
VARIANTS: Shanen, Shannon, Shanon

Shamir
Originating from the Hebrew for 'flint'.

Shelley
Originating in the Old English for 'wood near a ledge, clearing or meadow'.
VARIANTS: Shell, Shelly

Shem
In the Bible, Shem was one of Noah's sons, born to him when he was 500 years old.
VARIANTS: Shammas, Shemuel

Sheridan
Thought to be a Gaelic name meaning 'wild' or 'untamed', a development of 'Siridran'.
VARIANTS: Sheridon, Sherry

Sidney
From Old English this means 'from a riverside meadow', and also a contraction of the French 'St Denis'.
VARIANTS: Sid, Syd, Sydney

Silas
Derived from the Greek word for 'wood'.

Simon
Derived from the Greek for 'snub-nosed' and the Hebrew for 'God has heard', 'listening' and, oddly enough, 'little hyena'.
VARIANTS: Cimon, Imon, Sameir, Samer, Semon, Shimone, Si, Silas, Sim, Simao, Simeon, Simi, Simion, Simkin, Simone, Simp, Simpson, Sims, Sy, Symon

Sinclair
A contraction of Saint-Clair, the French place name borne by a Norman martyr.
VARIANTS: Clarence, Sinclaire, Sinclar

Sol
Meaning 'sun' in Latin, Sol is a short form of Solomon.

Solomon
Derived from the Hebrew word for 'peace', 'shalom'.
VARIANTS: Salaman, Salamon, Salman, Salo, Saloman, Salome, Salomo, Shelomo, Sol, Solmon.

Spencer
Derived from the Old French meaning 'dispenser of provisions' or 'administrator'.
VARIANTS: Spence, Spenser

Spike
Taken from the Latin 'spika', meaning a spiky point or an ear of corn.

Stacey
A short form of Eustace, derived from the Greek meaning 'rich in corn', 'fruitful' or a 'good harvest'.
VARIANTS: Stacie, Stacy

Stanley
Taken from the old German for a 'stony clearing'.
VARIANTS: Stan, Stanford, Stanleigh, Stanly, Stanton

Stephen
From the Greek meaning 'crown'.
VARIANTS: Steve, Steven

Sweeney
Derived from the Gaelic word meaning 'little hero'.

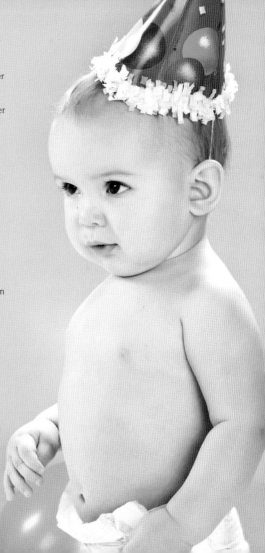

Tad

Anglicised form of the Gaelic name Tadhg, meaning 'poet' or 'philosopher'. Also a short form of Thaddeus, which may come from the Aramaic for 'praise, desired' or the Greek for 'gift of God'.
VARIANTS: Tadhg, Thaddeus, Theodore

Tariq

The Arabic meaning of Tariq is 'visitor'. In Hindi it means 'morning star'.

Tate

The Middle English meaning of this name is 'cheerful' or 'spirited'.
VARIANT: Tait

Terry

Short for Terence, the Anglicised form of the Irish Gaelic for 'initiator of an idea', or possibly from the Latin for 'to wear out' or 'to polish'.
VARIANTS: Tel, Telly, Terence, Terencio, Terrance, Terryal

Theo

A short form of Theobald, an Old French name that means 'bold people' and also Theodore, from the Greek for 'gift of God'.
VARIANTS: Tad, Tadd, Taddeus, Tebald, Ted, Tedd, Teddie, Teddy, Thadeus, Thebault, Theo, Theophilus, Thibaud, Thibault, Tibald, Tibold

Thomas

From the Aramaic and Greek for 'twin'.
VARIANTS: Tamas, Tom, Tomas, Tome, Tomm, Tommie, Tommy

Timothy

Derived from a Greek name that means 'honouring God'.
VARIANTS: Tim, Timmie, Timofey

Toby

A short form of the biblical name Tobias, which comes from the Hebrew for 'God is good'.
VARIANTS: Tobe, Tobey, Tobiah, Tobie, Tobin, Tobit, Tobye, Tobyn

Todd

Originally a surname, Todd comes from the Middle English for 'fox'.
VARIANTS: Tad, Tod, Toddie, Toddy

Travis

An English family name that comes from the Old French for 'a crossing'.
VARIANTS: Travers, Travon, Travus, Trevon

Walker
The Old English meaning of Walker is 'to tread'. It is a former occupational name used for 'a fuller of cloth'.
VARIANT: Wal

Warner
A medieval name that comes from the Old German for 'guard' and 'army'.
VARIANTS: Garnier, Warren, Werner, Wernher

Warren
Originally a surname brought to England by the French from the town of La Varenne.
VARIANTS: Varner, Ware, Waring, Warner, Warrener

Webster
An Old English occupational name for a 'weaver'.
VARIANTS: Web, Webb

Wesley
The Old English meaning of Wesley is 'western wood, meadow or clearing'.
VARIANTS: Lee, Leigh, Wellesley, Wes, Wesleigh, Wesly, Wezley

William
From the Germanic Wilhelm, meaning 'will, desire' and 'helmet, protection'.
VARIANTS: Bill, Billy, Guillaume, Liam, Wil, Wilem, Wilhelm, Williamson, Willie, Willy

Wycliffe
From the Old Norse for 'village near the cliff'.
VARIANTS: Wyche, Wyck, Wycke

Xavier
A popular French and Spanish name, taken from the Arabic meaning 'bright'.
VARIANTS: Javier, Zever

Yosef
A variant of the biblical name Joseph, which comes from the Hebrew for 'God will add (another son)'.
VARIANT: Joseph

Zachary
A variant of the biblical name Zachariah, which means 'remembrance of God'.
VARIANTS: Zac, Zachariah, Zack, Zechariah

Zakkai
From the Hebrew for 'pure, innocent'.

Zamir
From the Hebrew for 'song'.

Zion
A variant of Sion, which is the name of the hill on which the city of Jerusalem was built.

Trey

From the Latin for 'three'. Also a variant of the Cornish Tremaine, meaning 'the house on the rock'.
VARIANT: Tremaine

Tyler

An Old English occupational name for someone who tiled roofs or made tiles.
VARIANTS: Tiler, Ty, Tye

Tyrone

A county in Northern Ireland, Tyrone means 'Owen's country'.
VARIANTS: Ty, Tye, Tyron

Tyson

From the French for 'firebrand', this name was originally a nickname given to a bad-tempered person.
VARIANTS: Tie, Ty, Tye, Tysen, Tysone

Uri

The short form of Uriah, which means 'God is my light' in Hebrew.
VARIANTS: Uriah, Urie, Yuri

Valentine

See *Valentina* in the Girls' section.

Vaughan

From the Old Welsh for 'little'.
VARIANTS: Van, Vaughn, Vaune, Vawn, Vawne, Vonn

Victor

From the Latin for 'victory'.
VARIANTS: Vic, Vick, Victoir, Viktor, Vito, Vitor

Vincent

Derived from the Latin for 'conquering'.
VARIANTS: Vince, Vincente, Vine, Vinnie, Vinny, Vinson

Virgil

The name of a Roman poet, Virgil comes from the Latin for 'stick' and is thought to imply 'staff-bearer'.
VARIANTS: Verge, Vergit, Virge, Virgie, Virgilio

Vivian

See *Vivian* in the Girls' section.